Darwen In Its Hey Day

First edition 2010

Second edition
Heritage Publications, Blackburn, 2012

ISBN 978-0-9572604-4-3

More local history books available from our website:

Heritage Publications

www.HeritagePublications.co.uk

Darwen In Its Hey Day

This book is dedicated to David Waddicor.

David died recently and I would like to express my appreciation for his typesetting expertise, his advice on photography and for his patience and friendship.

L. Anne Hull

Darwen In Its Hey Day

THE INTENTION is to cover the interesting events and the people concerned with these events in Darwen in the Edwardian era and up to the First World War. However, it will begin at the end of the 19th century with the building of the Technical School, and a look at the monuments already erected in the Parks and the erection of the Tower which gives Darwen its identity.

The Edwardian era was, in the main, a time of prosperity and growth in the town of Darwen. In 1911 the population had increased to over forty thousand. Much garden fronted improved terraced housing was built to accommodate the growing workforce. Larger, grander houses were often built near the Parks.

In this short period of time there was the death of Queen Victoria and of King Edward VII, two Coronations and one Royal Visit. The people of Darwen were eager to celebrate royal occasions and commemorate them in various ways. There were many civic ceremonies involving these royal events, the opening of new buildings and the improvement in leisure facilities.

Information researched and assembled by
  L. Anne Hull

Designed and printed by
  David Waddicor

(MMIX/MMX)

Additional design and printing, 2012, Heritage Publications

www.HeritagePublications.co.uk

Acknowledgements

Thanks to the following for their kindness, generosity and support:

Mary Painter and the staff at Darwen Library

Alan Holden for several photographs

Harold Heys for use of the article on Albert Whalley and
other information

Brian Hilton for some photographs and information

Edwin C. Raine (aged 100 years) for his knowledge and interest in
Darwen which has been a source of inspiration

SOURCES

Local newspapers~Darwen Advertiser, Darwen News,
 Darwen Gazette

Barrett's Directories

Almanacs

Year Books

Alan Duckworth—"A Never to be Forgotten Day"

Annie Proctor—Darwen's Old School Tie

M. Rothwell—Industrial Heritage

J. Pomfret—Jubilee Souvenir

Gazette—Pictorial Darwen

Contents

1904
Blackburn Road Wesleyan Chapel opened
Café Chantant started
New museum and art gallery opened
Fish pond in Sunnyhurst Wood constructed

1905
The Potter Gateway built
Paddling Pool constructed in Sunnyhurst Wood

1906
Walpamur
Nurses Home moved to new premises
Sundial in Sunnyhurst Wood

1907
First Freeman of Darwen
Strike at Woodside Mill
Falcon Avenue entrance to Sunnyhurst Wood opened
Everton Street Bowling Club opened
Explosion at Earnsdale Bakery
Drinking Fountain in Sunnyhurst Wood and Gateway in Whitehall Park
presented
Hollins Grove Chapel constructed

1908
The New Free Library opened
Fire at India Mill
General Booth visited
St Cuthbert's Bell Tower
Baptist Church Jubilee
Falcon Avenue Gateway presented
Theatre Royal

1909
First Darwen Scout Group
Roller Skating

1910
Bull Hill Hospital opened new building
Darwen Industrial Co-operative Society Jubilee
Sudell Road School opened

1911

Sundial in Whitehall Park presented
Coronation of George V
Whitehall Park Gates
National rail strike
Consecration of St Barnabas Church

1912

Exhibition of paintings
Sunnyhurst Wood Tea Room opened
Presentation of Greenway Shelter
Earnsdale Cotton Waste Mill fire
The Huntington Bridge opened
Demonstration by Gustav Hamel

1913

Darwen jockey's narrow escape at Ascot
Royal visit of King George and Queen Mary

1914

Olympia Picture Palace opened
New Garden Village built
Spring Bank School opened
Jubilee of St John's Church
Moss Bridge Hospital

ASSOCIATIONS AND CLUBS

DATE STONES

PROMINENT PEOPLE

1890s

IN THIS SECTION

The Technical School

The Technical School and School of Art opened in 1894 and replaced the borough school in William Street. Mr C. P. Huntington laid the foundation stone in 1893 and gave £1,000 to be invested and to provide an annual prize. It was opened by Councillor Cocker, the Mayor, and it also housed the Education Offices and a public library.

The part of the building which was the Higher Grade School was opened by Dr Forsyth, principal of the Higher Grade School in Leeds. It opened with 81 scholars, 57 boys and 24 girls. Rawdon Roberts, B.Sc., was the first headmaster. The Co-op offered grants for free places.

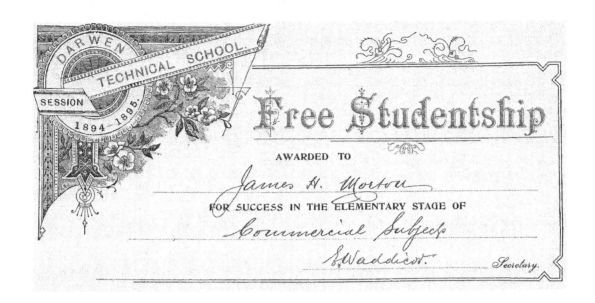

James Hargreaves Morton, the artist, was a pupil and he won a scholarship to study at the Royal College of Art. He was killed at the end of the First World War.

1881-1918

The Tower

I T WAS DECIDED that the town would commemorate Queen Victoria's Diamond Jubilee and the achievement of gaining access to the moors for the people of Darwen by erecting a building on the highest point in the town. David Ellison, a clerk in the Darwen Borough Engineer's Office and son of the Borough Treasurer, produced the winning design. R. W. Smith-Saville was appointed as architect and the plans were slightly modified.

The Lord of the Manor agreed to the erection of the tower on Darwen Hill and gave the whole of the stone used from the adjacent Red Delph quarry. The first sod was cut in 1897 by the Mayor Alexander Carus.

Sod cutting ceremony on Darwen Hill

On September 24th 1898, 3,000 people assembled for the opening by the Rev W. A. Duckworth, Lord of the Manor. Also on the platform were Councillor Carus and the Mayor Charles Huntington.

The tower is 86 feet high, octagonal in shape with walls 2 feet thick, 65 stone steps, 17 iron steps and 16 windows. Public subscriptions had raised £2,000 out of which £800 was used to construct the tower.

The Diamond Jubilee Committee voted for £650 of the fund to go to the Nursing Association to be invested and some of the income used to send patients to Convalescent Hospitals and the rest used for the general purposes of the Nursing Association.

Plaques on the walls of the tower state the reason why it was built—for the Diamond Jubilee and for gaining access to the moors.

1897

THIS TOWER

was erected (and a sum of £650

devoted in aid of the

nursing association) out of the

public subscriptions raised

to commemorate the

DIAMOND JUBILEE

of the reign of

HER MAJESTY

QUEEN VICTORIA

Foundation laid June 22nd 1897

by Alexander Carus Esq., J.P., Mayor

Opened September 24th 1898 by

The Rev. William Arthur Duckworth, M.A.
Lord of the Manor

Charles Philip Huntington Esq., J.P., Mayor

THE COMMITTEE

Chairman ALEXANDER CARUS, Esq., J.P., Mayor

Vice Chairman ALDERMAN JAMES COCKER

COUNCILLORS

J. W. Gillibrand, J.P
Captⁿ Rawlinson
T. W. A Forrest
John H. Wraith, J.P
Jos. J. Riley, J.P., C.C
W. Walmsley, J.P
Henry D. Ashton
Fred G. Hindle
Enoch Schofield

Robert Shorrock
Alfred Cooper
D. J Shackleton
Richard Holden
Heman Coulthurst
Aremena Coulthurst
G. Pickup Holden
Thomas Whalley
Harold Y. L. Smith

Thos. Stockdale

CHARLES COSTEKER   Town Clerk
Hon. Secretary

R. W. SMITH SAVILLE, G.E.   Borough Engineer
Hon. Architect

D. LLOYD JAMES   Assistant Secretary

RICHARD J. WHALLEY   Builder

22

Queen Victoria's Diamond Jubilee

CHILDREN IN THE town were given 2 days holiday from school. At Blackburn Road Wesleyan School, managers gave each child the New Testament. Each child received an orange on leaving school. There was a mass meeting of children in the Market Square. Children went back to school and were presented with a medal and 3 new pennies each.

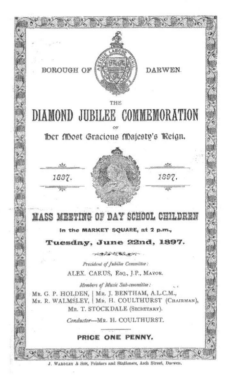

To the Inhabitants of the Borough of Darwen.

THE QUEEN'S DIAMOND JUBILEE.

At a Public Meeting, held in this Borough, the following Resolutions were passed:—

That a Committee be appointed to solicit Subscriptions, and make arrangements for Celebrating in Darwen the Long Reign of the Queen, on the following basis:—

(1) That nothing be added to the Permanent Expenses of the Town as a consequence of such Celebration.

(2) That the Day itself be Celebrated.

(3) That such other Commemorative Work or Ceremony be undertaken as the Committee may think fit.

(4) That the Surplus be applied in aid of the Funds for Nursing the Sick and Indigent Inhabitants of the Borough, and enabling those below the par line of health who are themselves unable to find the necessary funds to recover convalescence by means of change of air and scene.

The Members of the Committee are:—The Mayor; Aldermen Cocker and Eccles; Councillors Cooper, Forrest, Gillibrand, Rawlinson, and Shackleton; Dr. John H. Wraith; Messrs. H. D. Ashton, J. J. Riley, F. G. Hindle, T. Whalley, W. Atkinson, Robert Shorrock, W. Walmsley, A. Coulthurst, H. Y. L. Smith, T. Stockdale, F. Arthur Yeo, Enoch Schofield, G. P Holden, Richard Holden (Blackburn), and Heman Coulthurst.

The Committee above referred to met on the 29th April, and they desired me to bring under your notice the Commemorative Arrangements proposed to be carried out in Darwen, in addition to which I intend myself to set apart a day for Entertaining the Aged Inhabitants.

The Committee have decided that on the 22nd day of June, a Fête of the Day School Scholars should be held, at which provision will be made for Amusements and Refreshments, and each child will, in addition, be presented with a Commemoration Medal, and Music will also be supplied; and in the Evening there will be Illuminations and a Bon-Fire on Darwen Moor. The Scholars will assemble in the Market Square at 2 p.m. and will sing the Old Hundred and another hymn to the tune of "Edwinston" and the National Anthem.

The Committee further propose, if their funds will allow, to perpetuate the unique occasion by erecting a Tower, 100 feet in height, on the most elevated portion of the Moor, subject to all necessary consents being first obtained. From this Tower a commanding view will be had of the surrounding country—including Blackpool, Morecambe Bay, and the Cumberland and Yorkshire Hills. The estimated cost is £1,250.

We hope to obtain a handsome surplus in aid of that most useful Institution, namely, our Nursing Association.

As you are well aware the success of all the arrangements necessarily depends on the public spirit shown by the inhabitants, and the amount of Donations received by the Committee, and I am, therefore, to ask you for your kind support and aid. Subscriptions can be paid to any Member of the Committee; the Hon. Treasurer, Mr. Whalley, at the County Bank; or to any of the other local Banks.

Subscriptions may also be paid to the 1s. Funds kindly opened by the *Darwen News* and *Darwen Post* and the *Advertiser* 6d. Fund. Subscribers should state to what Fund (Tower or Nurses) they wish their money applied to.

I hope the proposed arrangements will meet with your approval, and that you will mark your sense of the occasion by subscribing to such worthy objects in Commemoration of the 60th Year of Her Most Gracious Majesty's Reign.

Your obedient servant,

ALEXANDER CARUS,
MAYOR.

N. Leach, Printer, "Advertiser" Office, Darwen.

1837.  **1897.**

BOROUGH OF DARWEN.

Programme.

OF

DIAMOND JUBILEE

COMMEMORATION PROCEEDINGS.

TUESDAY, JUNE 22nd, 1897.

a.m.
8 to 8-30.—Holy Trinity Church Bells Chime.
Queen's Change and Shooting.

9-30 to 10-30.—Holy Trinity Church Bells Chime.
Grandsire Peal.

9-45—Volunteers "fall in" Review Order. Band and Drums.

10-0—Music by Temperance Band, on the Market Square.
Assembly at Municipal Buildings for Civic Procession to Holy Trinity Church.

10-15—Civic Procession from Municipal Buildings to Holy Trinity Church.
ORDER OF PROCESSION :

1—Police.	6—Volunteers.
2—Postmen.	7—Corporate Officials.
3—Fire Brigade.	8—Town Councillors.
4—General Public.	9—Deputy-Mayor.
5—Magistrates.	

10-20.— CHURCH SERVICE.
Overture from " The Messiah " (*Handel*)..ORCHESTRAL BAND.
10-30—QUEEN'S SONG .. Choir .... (*Eaton Fanning*.)
" For this great reign now rounded,
To three score of golden years."

Exhortation. Confession. Absolution. Lord's Prayer. Versicles. Psalm xx. First Lesson : Proverbs viii., 1—17. Te Deum (Jackson) in F. Second Lesson : 1 Peter ii., 6—18. Apostles' Creed. Salutations. Special Suffrages from the Accession Service. Collects.
Anthem......"The Hallelujah Chorus" ('Mount of Olives')
(*Beethoven*).
Special Prayers for the Queen and Royal Family. Prayer for Unity of the Universal Church. General Thanksgiving. Special Thanksgiving for the Queen.

Hymn (by desire of the Queen) :
" O King of Kings, whose reign of old
Hath been from everlasting."

Short Sermon by the Vicar. Offertories for the Nurses' Home, during which the Orchestral Band will play " The Pastoral Symphony," from " The Messiah."
Anthem...." Lift up your heads "(" Messiah ") ..(*Handel*)

The Congregation will sing—
"God Save the Queen."
Benediction.
Voluntary by the Orchestral Band......Coronation March from " La Prophete " (*Meyerbeer*).
The Clergy of Holy Trinity and St. James's are expected to conduct the Service, and the Lessons will be read by the Revs. R. Nicholls and E. Knibbs.
Mr. G. P. Holden will preside at the organ. Mr. J. Bentham, A.L.C.M., and Mr. G. Butterworth will conduct the musical portion of the service.

The Volunteers discharged their
rifles in honour of the Queen

The crowd gathered
in the Market
Square for the
celebrations

This banner stretched
across Bridge Street

The Parks

IN 1900 DARWEN already had two parks: Whitehall, opened in 1879 and Bold Venture, opened in 1887 with an extension opened in 1898.

WHITEHALL PARK

The Lightbown fountain was erected in 1886, the donor being the Mayoress, Mrs. T. Lightbown. This was the first ornament erected in any of the parks.

Mrs. T. Lightbown

Circa 1900

Erected 1886

The Pickup Bandstand was erected by the Pickup family in memory of Alderman Pickup, J.P., in 1897. It also commemorated Queen Victoria's Diamond Jubilee.

BOLD VENTURE PARK

The Huntington fountain was erected in 1896 as a memorial to James Huntington. The work people of Belgrave Mills subscribed £500 in memory of their esteemed employer. It was demolished for its metal to be used in World War II.

The Rutherford Band Stand was erected in 1895. It was the gift of Mr. John Rutherford, M.P., for Darwen.

The Gillibrand Observatory was erected in 1897. It was the Diamond Jubilee gift of Councillor J. W. Gillibrand.

OTHER EVENTS

1890s

1893   Bolton Road
        Congregational Chapel
        opened on November 2nd

THE ORIGINAL CHURCH BUILDING
(Demolished in 1952)

1894-97 Hollins Sewerage Works constructed

1896   Freeing of Darwen Moors

1897   Model Lodging House erected (Opened 1898)

        Industrial Hall opened on February 27th

1898   W. B. Huntington commenced duties as High Sheriff of Lancashire
on April 18th (see Prominent People section for photograph)
        YMCA established on May 2nd

1900

IN THIS SECTION

Darwen Gazette

THE FIRST DARWEN GAZETTE was on sale to the public on Friday January 5th, taking the place of the Darwen Post. This was because there was a change in the proprietorship of the Bankside

Printing Works and it was felt desirable that a change should be made in the name and to a very large extent in the general arrangements of the paper. The cost of the paper was 1d. For a period of time, from November 14th 1903 to October 1st 1910 it was known as the "Darwen and Country Gazette", which was a Conservative newspaper.

The Gazette building is situated on Borough Road and was designed by Messrs Stones and Stones of Blackburn. As well as providing accommodation for the business there were four lock-up shops facing Borough Road. The office entrance was in Borough Road and the Goods entrance and workmen's entrance was in Bank Bottoms. Electricity was installed to drive the

machinery and to produce the lighting, by Messrs G. H. Woods and Co., of Darwen and Blackburn working in conjunction with Messrs Holmes and Co., of Newcastle. A Webb printing machine was erected, capable of turning out 24,000 copies an hour.

The materials used for the exterior of the structure are facing bricks from Messrs Whittaker's kilns at Mill Hill, Yorkshire Stone and Kirkby Ireleth Slates. The contractor for the building work was Mr John Knowles of Darwen.

The Beginning of the Boer War

EOPLE IN DARWEN were always eager to celebrate National events, often leaving work and gathering in the centre of the town. The principal victories won by the British Army in South Africa were made the subject of special rejoicing.

Pretoria Day, when Pretoria was taken from the Boers, was celebrated on June 7th 1900. Also celebrated were the relief of Ladysmith on February 28th and Mafeking on May 18th.

Captain Arthur Huntington, son of W. B. Huntington, volunteered and was accepted by the Duke of Lancaster's Yeomanry. On

Pretoria Day and the one below

January 17th the Volunteers had a public send off, the men being entertained to dinner at the Millstone Hotel by the Mayor and afterwards a

public entertainment was given in the Co-operative Hall. The men left England aboard the *Doune Castle* on February 11th.

Private Bland was the first "Darrener" to lose his life in the war. The Boer War lasted from 1899 to 1902 when peace was declared on May 31st.

The Volunteers on parade in the Market Square

The news reached Darwen between 9-30 and 10 o'clock and in a short time the mills had emptied, the streets were ablaze with colours and bells rang out with joyous peals.

"Jimmy Tockus" (James Duxbury)
Celebrating Ladysmith Day

The Darwen Volunteer Barracks (Everton Street)

Spring Vale Railway Accident

THIS WAS A SERIOUS accident but happily without loss of life and though there was danger involved, it did have its humorous side.

On January 27th a goods train left Entwistle station on its way to Darwen. En route it was stopped approaching a dip so that pin brakes could be applied on each wagon. For this purpose the entire crew left the train to carry out the work. At this moment the whole train began to move downhill under its own weight. The fireman and the guard managed to leap into the guard's van before the train rushed through Sough tunnel at 40 mph with no one at the controls. At Spring Vale a second goods train was about to move off to Blackburn. Luckily the

guard was not on board when the runaway train crashed into it. As a result of the collision the track was torn up and skips of cotton tossed about like shuttlecocks.

The unfortunate driver who was stranded south of the tunnel, set off to follow the train on foot, smashing his lamp and tripping and falling going through the tunnel. He emerged to view a scene of devastation, but luckily with no loss of life. The track had been torn up, wagons were in splinters, and the misbehaving engine lay on its side.

General Election Day

THIS ELECTION (October 11th) was contested between John Rutherford (Conservative), who lived at Beardwood, Blackburn, and Charles Philip Huntington (Liberal), who lived at Astley Bank, Darwen.

It was known as a khaki election because at this time the Boer War was a major issue. The Liberals were opposed to the war, but the Conservatives supported the troops and there was a strong feeling of patriotism at this time.

Darwen was a large constituency taking in many outlying areas.

In Darwen itself there was plenty of support for C. P. Huntington (Liberal), but the Conservatives won with a majority of 470.

Colonel Sir John Rutherford. Bart.

No. of Votes 7,228

C. P. HUNTINGTON, Esq., J.P.

No. of Votes 6,758

Electric Trams

THE TRAM SERVICE began in Darwen in 1881 (October 16th) from the Angel Inn at the Circus to Blackburn and it was steam powered. It was the first fully steam powered line in the country.

Electrification work started in 1899 and the makers of the cars were George Milne & Co., of Shropshire. At first they were open-topped but because of the climate closed tops became standard. They could seat 60 passengers and were painted red and cream, running from Whitehall to Blackburn, starting in 1900.

It was noted that: "Their appearance in the streets is a pleasing ornament to the not too many pleasant features of our town,

whilst

the illuminations at night caused quite a number of pennies to be expended on trips from one stage to another during the early days of their career." (*Darwen Year Book*)

All tram services discontinued in 1946.

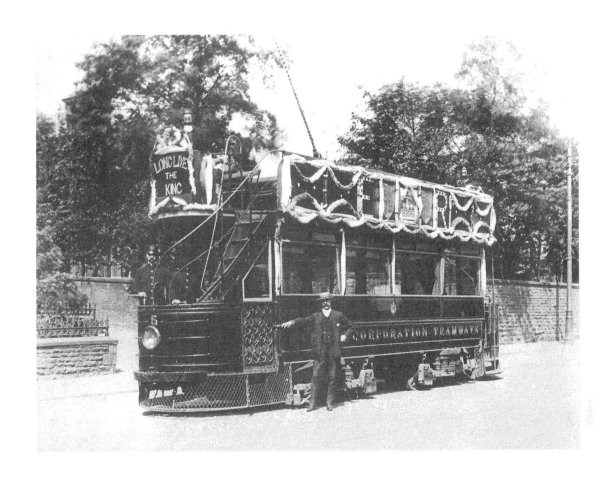

The tram above is decorated for the Coronation of Edward VII. Unlike Darwen, Blackburn was reluctant to decorate their trams.

The "Tory" Co-op

THE TOWN'S Conservatives formed the Provident Co-operative Society in competition with the original Co-operative Society.

In 1900 the new central premises were opened situated on the Green. The large building had grocery, tailoring, dressmaking, millinery and footwear departments, offices and a meeting hall above the store, able to hold 350 people.

Messrs Sames and Green were the architects and the building was opened by John Rutherford, M.P. on November 10th.

It closed after the First World War.

Market Hall Clock

DR. JAMES TODD BALLANTYNE donated the clock to commemorate his year as Mayor in 1898-99 at a cost of £150. The Market Hall was opened on June 21st, 1882 by Mr F. W. Grafton, M.P. It was built in Queen Anne style at a cost of £31,000, including cost of the site which was £11,000.

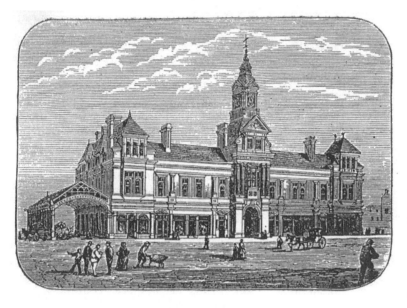

The clock was manufactured by Potts & Co., of Leeds, and was throughout of the very best quality. The bell weighed 6 cwt., and was made of the best metal.

There were 4 white dials, each 3 feet 4 inches in diameter, and the hands were made of copper. It would go 8 days with one winding and it was guaranteed not to vary more than ¼ minute in 3 months. It was

automatically lighted depending on the season. It was started on Monday, March 5th 1900.

The Market Hall before 1900 (no clock)

The Market Hall early 1900

The clock tower today (2009) showing the bell at the School Street side

Darwen Football Club

DARWEN FOOTBALL CLUB moved from Barley Bank to the Anchor Ground in 1900. The playing pitch was on land attached to Anchor Farm. Dick Smith, the tenant, loaned the club £100 to save the stand at Barley Bank from demolition. The money was used to transport it to the Anchor.

Barley Bank Football Ground

In the season 1898-99, Darwen Football Club Ltd., collapsed and the club exited from League football. It was decided after several meetings that a new club entirely should be formed and should join the Lancashire League and enter Lancashire and English Cup Competitions. Mr A. W. Huntington became president of the new venture and they soon got a team of youngsters together from the locality.

In 1901-02 they won the East Lancashire Charity Cup and the Lancashire League Championship. Medals were presented by Captain Huntington.

This Darwen team in 1901-1902 won the East Lancashire Charity Cup (seen in the photograph) and the Lancashire League championship, going through the season without defeat.
Back (left to right): Mr Will Todd (committee), J.Bridge (right half), J. Haslam (right back), Arnott (goal), Mr (now Alderman) W. Knowles (chairman), B. Pomfret (left back), G. Pollard (left half), Mr R. Eccles (secretary).
Front: P. Duckworth (outside right), D. Cooper (inside right), Walker (centre half), J Hulligan (centre-forward), P. Quinn (inside left), C. Dawson (outside left).

Electricity Works and Refuse Destructor

THE ELECTRICITY PLANT was built at Robin Bank and opened in 1899 on September 27th by the Mayor, Dr Ballantyne. It comprised four engines with a total of 1,500 horse power. Electricity was now needed for the tram cars and for street lighting.

A refuse destructor was built nearby and came into operation the following year. It was one of the most up to date plants in the country. This combined scheme aimed to utilise the waste heat produced by the destruction of refuse to make steam for the electricity works, called the Meldrum System. Tin cans, iron etc., were sorted out and sold and the remainder used to make steam.

The residue was carted to tips in a sterilized condition. Investigations proved the scheme was practicable and reduced the costs of disposing of the town's refuse.

Entrance to Tipping Shed.

Tipping Floor—Cart Dumping Refuse into Hopper.

Interior of Refuse Destructor House at Darwen.

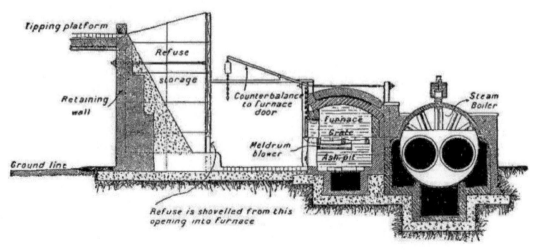

The Meldrum System

48

OTHER EVENTS

A Fire at Provident Mill causing damage costing £2,000 on March 18th

General Booth of the Salvation Army visits on June 11th

1901

IN THIS SECTION

Memorial Service for Queen Victoria

Official proclamation of Edward VII as King

Golf Club pavilion opened

Tramway to Hoddlesden opened

Aviary in Bold Venture Park presented

Present Darwen Cricket Club founded

Death of Queen Victoria

(January 22nd)

THE MEMORIAL SERVICE was held in the Wesley (Wesleyan) Chapel (Railway Road) on February 2nd 1901.

STATE ATTENDANCE
OF
HIS WORSHIP THE MAYOR & CORPORATION
AT
MEMORIAL SERVICE
FOR
HER LATE MAJESTY THE QUEEN,
IN WESLEY CHAPEL, DARWEN, FEBRUARY 2ND, 1901.

Order of Service.

HYMN I.

O GOD! our help in ages past,
Our hope for years to come,
Our shelter from the stormy blast,
And our eternal home.

Under the shadow of thy throne,
Still may we dwell secure;
Sufficient is thine arm alone,
And our defence is sure.

Before the hills in order stood,
Or earth received her frame,
From everlasting thou art God,
To endless years the same.

A thousand ages in thy sight
Are like an evening gone,
Short as the watch that ends the night
Before the rising sun.

The busy tribes of flesh and blood,
With all their cares and fears,
Are carried downward by the flood,
And lost in following years.

Time, like an ever-rolling stream,
Bears all its sons away;
They fly forgotten, as a dream
Dies at the opening day.

O God! our help in ages past,
Our hope for years to come,
Be thou our guard while life shall last,
And our perpetual home.

PRAYER ... ... REV. GEORGE HACK.

HYMN 2.

ROCK of ages, cleft for me,
Let me hide myself in thee;
Let the water and the blood,
From thy wounded side which flowed,
Be of sin the double cure,
Save from wrath and make me pure.

Could my tears for ever flow,
Could my zeal no langour know,

These for sin could not atone;
Thou must save and thou alone:
In my hand no price I bring,
Simply to thy cross I cling.

While I draw this fleeting breath,
When my eyes shall close in death,
When I rise to worlds unknown,
And behold thee on thy throne,
Rock of ages, cleft for me,
Let me hide myself in thee.

The Wesleyan Chapel was opened in 1866 and the architect was Ernest Bates who was also the architect for India Mill. The contractor was John Knowles who constructed many important buildings in Darwen.

Wesleyan Chapel, Railway Road

Saturday was regarded as the day of mourning. Mills and workshops closed all day. Public houses closed at noon, some for several hours and some for the rest of the day. Black was worn and blinds were lowered. At 2 o'clock the civic procession formed at the Municipal Chambers to accompany the Mayor to the Wesleyan Chapel. The procession was one of the largest seen in Darwen and the streets were lined with people. A united memorial service was held at the Wesleyan Chapel and also at Holy Trinity Church. Both churches were crowded and hundreds were turned away.

Proclamation of the King

THE PHOTOGRAPH SHOWS the official proclamation of Edward VII as King. It took place outside the Angel Inn at the Circus by the Mayor Councillor John Tomlinson on January 28th 1901 at 1 o'clock and several thousand people assembled.

The Mayor mounted a waggonette. Several buglers who occupied the front seat gave a call and hats were removed by the people, then the National Anthem was sung. The officials drank to the health of the King and Queen at the Municipal Buildings.

New Pavilion for Darwen Golf Club

THE GOLF CLUB originated in 1893. At this time members had to use rooms hired at a local farm for changing rooms. In 1900 it was decided to purchase a club house from Fairfield Golf Club in Manchester.

This was bought using donations and gifts from members and was soon decorated and equipped to a high standard. It was opened in 1900 and

funds were made available to develop a garden and shrubbery and a putting green was constructed at the side of the Clubhouse.

An extension was built and the Clubhouse was formally opened on May 11th, 1901 by Rev. A. T. Corfield, Vicar of Tockholes and a pioneer of the game in the district. There was a very good gathering of ladies and gentlemen and music was performed by members of the Lyric Band.

Mr F. G. Hindle, who proposed a vote of thanks to Mr Corfield in a humorous speech, said the members had selected that

gentleman to perform the opening ceremony because he introduced that delightful game into the district. As one who previously had taken part in more violent games he (Mr Hindle) first scoffed at the game, but remained to play it. People played golf for all sorts of reasons. There was the gentleman who played to reduce his weight, another who played for a thirst—(Laughter)—and still another who played so that he might wear a gay costume. (Laughter). There were also people who played it as an exercise. (Hear, hear.) All these were innocent and some were meritorious. However, if the advice given them by the captain to join that club were acted upon no one would be the worse for it. (Hear, hear, and applause).

The Tramway to Hoddlesden

THIS TRAMWAY ROUTE was opened on October 12th 1901 and was about one and a half miles long. It went along Bridge Street, up Sudell Road and Marsh House Lane, and over the moors to Hoddlesden. There was a problem about what type of car to use on this hilly journey. Eventually two lightweight, four wheeled, open top double-decker cars were ordered with a dual braking system - magnetic and

mechanical. Laying the track started in July 1901 and the two vehicles arrived on September 6th.

On October 12th a specially decorated car with the Mayor officiating as driver proceeded to the village of Hoddlesden where it was received by Col. W. H. Place and Councillor A. Carus. There was a welcoming party of schoolchildren, prominent citizens

and the Pickup Bank Brass Band assembled in Queen's Square.

There was a lunch at Hoddlesden Hall, home of Councillor A. Carus for the Mayor, Corporation and guests.

This was the menu:

Soup:
Mock Turtle

Fish:
Turbot   Sole

Entrees:
Stewed kidney   Mushrooms
Snipe pudding

Joints:
Ribs of beef   Saddle of mutton

Fowl:
Pheasant   Partridge

Pudding:
Tramway pudding
Cheese   Biscuits

Dessert:
Pears   Pine Apples   Grapes   Almonds
Raisins   Coffee

Wines:
Champagne–Roederer 1893
White wine–Vin de Graves
Burgundy–Spanish Don Quixote
Cigars

There was an accident in April 1926 when a tram failed to negotiate the sharp turn at the bottom of Sudell Road after losing control on a wet day.

The tram lines at the bottom of Sudell Road turning into Bridge Street

The Aviary in Bold Venture Park

ON NOVEMBER 1st 1901 Mr and Mrs F. Hindle presented the aviary in Bold Venture Park to commemorate their silver wedding anniversary.

There were about 150 birds in the aviary from various countries and they were kept under as nearly as possible natural

conditions. The aviary was designed by R. W. Smith-Saville, the Borough Engineer.

Today it is no longer there, in its place there is a metal pergola and a cobblestone mosaic.

Present Darwen Cricket Club Founded

IN THE NINETEENTH century cricket was played in Darwen on the Barley Bank ground. This was sold by the Lord of the Manor at the end of the century. On December 30th 1901 a group of friends met with a view to forming a cricket club. It was proposed that it should be called Darwen Etrurians. At the first annual general meeting on April 1st 1902 it was decided that they should join the Darwen League and a ground was obtained at Moss Farm.

The first match was away against the United Methodists at the Ironworks ground. The Etrurians won by 3 wickets and finished the first season fourth in the League. They won the Darwen League in 1903 and in 1904/05 a new ground was obtained at Birch Hall, the present ground of Darwen Cricket Club.

Original Darwen Cricket Club squad

OTHER EVENTS

St John Ambulance founded–headquarters in George Street

W. P. Halliwell became Town Clerk

Severe thunder storms on July 21st

> *Alexandra Hotel struck by lightning*

A contingent of active service men returned home to a great welcome

Darwen Industrial Co-operative Society transferred their bakery in Bolton Road, built in 1872, to new premises in Borough Road

1902

IN THIS SECTION

Kiosk erected in Bold Venture Park

New bridges constructed in Bold Venture Park

Coronation of Edward VII

Shorrock Fountain erected in Bold Venture Park

Catlow Fountain erected in Whitehall Park

Tramway Waiting Rooms built

The Kiosk in Bold Venture Park

THE KIOSK, WHICH was opened on January 23rd 1902, was donated by Mr and Mrs H. D. Ashton, it could accommodate 50 people. It was to be used as a tea house and the rent received was expected to be sufficient for its maintenance.

There was some controversy about it opening on a Sunday with many objections on religious grounds.

2009

New Bridges in Bold Venture Park

THE RUSTIC BRIDGES in Bold Venture Park were in need of repair. Mr Thomas Knowles, J.P., very generously paid for the erection of three new bridges to be built in a substantial manner.

Mr Knowles also invested a sum of £120 in Corporation Stock to form an endowment for their future maintenance. They were built to commemorate the Coronation of Edward VII and opened on March 19th 1902.

Today the inscription cannot be seen

Celebrations for the Coronation Of Edward Seventh

UNFORTUNATELY THE Coronation had to be postponed from June to August 9th 1902 due to the ill health of the King. (He had an appendectomy).

Darwen went ahead with the celebrations in June, many events having been planned. Many buildings in the town were decorated with bunting, flags and royal mottos. The bonfire on the moors was delayed until the actual Coronation.

The Procession leaving the Market Ground at 11-00 a.m. on Thursday 26th June

The service on the Market Ground on Thursday 26th June

For full content see Darwen Reference Library

The festivities took place over a period of four days, starting on Wednesday 25th June and finishing on Saturday 28th June. The main event was on Thursday with a procession going along Market Street, Duckworth Street as far as Bright Street then back to Mill Gap. It then returned to the Market Ground for a service. The Mayor (Mr Tomlinson) read a telegram from London saying that Edward was in a satisfactory condition. Afterwards the Mayor and guests went to the Co-operative Industrial Hall for a light lunch.

In the afternoon of Friday 27th June, the children from the town's schools assembled on the Market Ground. The Pickup Bank Band played and the Mayor gave a speech saying he hoped the weather would be good for the Gala the next day.

The Mayor went to Bold Venture Park to plant a commemorative oak tree and to accept the gifts of the Kiosk (Mr and Mrs H. D. Ashton) and of the Aviary (Mr and Mrs F. Hindle).

In the evening a fairy fountain played on the Market Ground, illuminated by a circle of electric lights.

The children were given Coronation mugs and medals. There was a distribution of food to aged people.

Edward VII on Obverse of 1902 Coronation Medallion

Queen Alexandra on Reverse of 1902 Coronation Medallion

Many buildings in the town were beautifully decorated

The Wesleyan Methodist Chapel in Railway Road

Six pillars were covered with royal scarlet cloth and entwined with wreaths of roses. Another band of cloth across the top of the building was festooned with flowers.

Bridge Street (Looking towards the Circus)

Bolton Road

Darwen Advertiser Office (N. Leach Ltd)

Coronation Decorations
1st Prize Winner
Belgrave Road

Coronation Decorations
2nd Prize Winner
Greenway Street

The Shorrock Drinking Fountain

IN COMMEMORATION OF the Coronation of Edward VII, Councillor Robert Shorrock, J.P., the Parks Chairman, presented a drinking fountain to Bold Venture Park. It was supplied with water from an adjoining spring.

2009

The Catlow Fountain

MESSRS JOHN CATLOW AND SONS presented the ornamental iron fountain which stands in the upper portion of Whitehall Park in commemoration of the Coronation of Edward VII. It cost £120 and water was obtained from a spring running through the Park. It had a basin with 4 cups, a canopy with eight columns making arches over which are placed royal figures.

Drawn around 1900

Catlow Fountain 2009 (before its renovation)

Tramway Waiting Rooms

BELGRAVE SQUARE WAS AN unsightly dumping ground before the building of the tramway waiting rooms. Mr F. G. Hindle offered £100 for the planting of shrubs and flowering trees in the Square. So to commemorate the Coronation of

Edward VII the Corporation decided to build elaborate underground conveniences and tramway waiting rooms and plant the back portion with the trees.

The waiting rooms were designed by the Borough Engineer, R. W. Smith-Saville and there was a parcel office at the rear. The Boer War memorial was included in the scheme and built later. The waiting rooms started to be used on January 1st, 1903.

The commemorative plaque on the side of the waiting rooms

Clearing the ground getting ready to build the waiting rooms

OTHER EVENTS

Honorarium of £200 granted to Mr R. W. Smith-Saville, Borough Engineer, in consideration of his work on behalf of the Hoddlesden tramway on January 6th

End of the Boer War on May 31st and peace declared. Rejoicings on June 4th

Darwen Volunteers welcomed home on June 21st and July 4th

David Shackleton became Member of Parliament for Clitheroe on July 1st. He was the first Labour member to be returned unopposed

Mr Balfour's Education Act handed the responsibility for Secondary Schools to the Lancashire County Council

Smallpox outbreak in December

1903

IN THIS SECTION

21ST Anniversary of the Literary Society

Boer War Memorial

Hollins Grove Conservative Club opened

Duckworth Street Congregational Chapel Jubilee

Sunnyhurst Wood opened

St. Georges Church consecrated

Fire at Moss Bridge Mill

21st Anniversary of the Literary Society

THE SOCIETY WAS founded so that the adult section of the community should be afforded opportunities of bettering their literary and scientific knowledge. This took the form of meetings

Presidents of the Society in this era

Mr. J. F. Leach, J.P.
President, 1899-1900.

Mr. George Yates, J.P.
President, 1900-1.

Mr. Geo. P. Holden, J.P.
President, 1901-2.

at which a paper was read by a member followed by a discussion. Meetings were held in the local Masonic Hall in Parliament Street until 1908 after which the meetings were held in the Library Rooms.

The 21st session of the Society in 1903 was regarded as an auspicious event and Alderman Timothy Lightbown, J.P., was recalled to the

Mr. H. A. Champion.
President, 1903-4.

Mr. J. J. Beckett.
President, 1904-5.

Mr. C. J. Beckett, J.P.
President, 1905-6.

Presidency. There were 131 members. Two debates were held in this session, on "The American Civil War" and "The Influence of the Press."

The great event was the Coming of Age Banquet which was held in the Industrial Hall on March 21st, when 114 members and 10 guests were present. The principal guest was Mr George Milner, M.A., President of the Manchester Literary Club.

The dinner was served soon

Mr. W. P. Kay.
President, 1906-7.
Hon. Secretary, 1884-90.

Mr. T. Y. Nuttall, J.P.
President, 1907-8.

Mr. T. E. Holgate, J.P.
B.Sc.
President, 1908-9.

Mr. Alex. MacIvor.
President, 1909-10.

Mr. F. J. Hamilton.
President, 1910-11.

Mr. R. H. Baldwin, J.P.
President, 1911-12.

after 7 o'clock and the tables were attractively adorned with beautiful flowers and greenery.

The menu was as follows:

Soup
Clear   Oxtail

Fish
Halibut   Shrimp Sauce

Entrees
Calf's Head   Kidneys and Mushrooms

Removes
Roast Ribs of Beef   Ducks   Chickens

Vegetables
New Potatoes   Spring Cabbage   Peas

Sweets
Apple Pudding   Rhubarb Tart
Custard

Cheese   Biscuits

There were toasts and musical items. Mr J. R. Williamson, a local poet, read an appropriate and lengthy ode, a beautifully decorated copy of

Mr. T. P. Davies, J.P.
President, 1912-13.

Mr. R. W. Smith-Saville,
A.M.I.C.E.
President, 1913-14.

Mr. W. P. Halliwell, B.A.
President, 1914-15.

which was generously presented to each gentleman present as the gift of Mr J. J. Riley. An example of this is in Darwen Reference Library.

Boer War Memorial

T THE END OF 1899 and soon after the outbreak of war in South Africa, a parade of the Darwen companies of the 1st Volunteers Brigade East Lancashire Regiment took place and the call for volunteers for active service met with immediate response.

On January 17th 1900 the Mayor entertained to dinner the local officers and men accepted for foreign service and a month later the contingent sailed for South Africa. During the course of the war the relief of Ladysmith and Mafeking and other victories occasioned impromptu rejoicings in the town.

On June 10th 1901, when the first contingent of active service men returned home, the town was en fete and the men were given a great welcome home. A similar tribute was given to a second contingent on its return a year later.

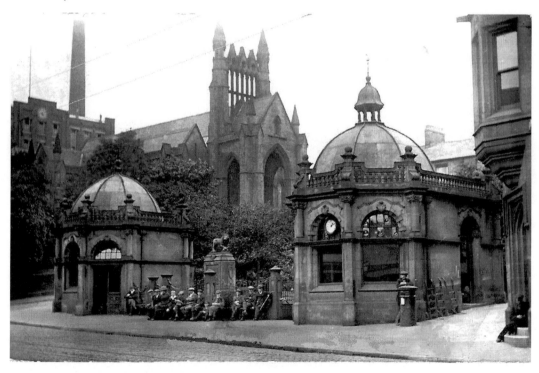

There were 14 men from Darwen who were killed in the war. It was decided to erect a memorial to those who fell and to those who gave their services. This was generously given by Alderman John Tomlinson and unveiled on Saturday 18th April 1903.

Unveiling of the Darwen War Memorial on Saturday 18th April 1903 by the Mayor and Mayoress, Mr and Mrs Robert Shorrock, J.P

2009

Hollins Grove Conservative Club

THE CLUB ORIGINATED in 1876 and the following year leased premises next to the George Hotel for their meetings. Prominent Conservatives in the town at this time were the Rev. Charles Greenway, Mr J. Huntington, Mr W. B. Huntington, Mr J. W. Gillibrand, Mr W. Walmsley and the Rev. P. Graham, all of whom gave their full support to the club. In 1900 it was decided that a new building was required for the club and in 1901 land was purchased from the

Rev. C. Greenway for this purpose. The club was opened on Saturday 27th June 1903 by Mr Rutherford, M.P. It was raining hard and too wet for speeches outside. The leaders of the party were present in full force with

the Chairman of the Division, Mr Adam Dugdale, presiding.

The key was presented to Mr Rutherford by Mr Hopkinson, the President of the club. In his speech Mr Rutherford made a most important statement as to his attitude on the question of the fiscal policy of the Empire, supporting Tariff Reform and against Free Trade. This part of the proceedings took place in the spacious assembly hall and afterwards there was a concert in the billiard room.

There were 300 members who paid a subscription of five shillings per year. Mr Rutherford gave a donation of £100 and a loan of £1,500. The full contract for the premises, including furniture and other items was nearly £2,250 and the contractor was Mr Thomas Lightbown.

Duckworth Street Congregational Chapel Jubilee

ON SATURDAY EVENING, 20th June, there was a social meeting preceded by tea in celebration of the Jubilee presided over by Rev W. C. Russell, M.A. The tea rooms were crowded with members of the congregation, past and present and Sunday Scholars of today and yesterday. In the Lecture Room the walls were adorned with portraits of departed friends of the Church and congregation.

The Rev Dr Brown of Bedford, who was to conduct the service on Sunday, was warmly welcomed. Dr Brown preached in the morning and in the evening. In the afternoon, the Duckworth Street and Highfield Schools met in the Chapel and were addressed by Mr J. H. Yates of Hale, Cheshire and by Mr E. M. Davies, a former Sunday School Superintendent who gave a stimulating talk.

1853. 1903.

JUBILEE ANNIVERSARY.

SATURDAY, · JUNE · 20th, · 1903.

Duckworth Street Congregational Chapel,

DARWEN.

The Opening of Sunnyhurst Wood

DARWEN IS GEOGRAPHICALLY A long and narrow town. At this time it already possessed two excellent parks, one at the southern end and one in the middle of the town. It was felt that the more populous northern end of the town should also have its own park. Sunnyhurst Wood seemed an ideal area for conversion to a public park.

The land had originally belonged to Mr Henry Brock Hollinshead and used for hunting. He sold it to Eccles Shorrock and it was from his descendants that the Corporation took it over. The Mayor at that time, Alderman John Tomlinson was very enthusiastic for the Wood to become a public park and proposed the scheme should go ahead in commemoration of the Coronation of Edward VII. Alderman Tomlinson launched a subscription fund to raise the estimated cost of £2,000.

The money would be needed for legal costs, the laying out of roads and footpaths, the purchase of railings, the buying and planting of shrubs, trees and wild flowers, and for drainage. It was initially thought that the land would be given free but this was not the case and the acquisition of the land cost the town £4,000. Part of the land was originally intended to be used as a reservoir but this did not happen. Much praise went to Alderman Tomlinson for securing the wood for the benefit of the public.

The Woods were declared officially open just below the gateway on Tockholes Road

On Thursday 2nd July 1903 at 3-30 pm, a large company met at the Old English Gateway on Tockholes Road, the main entrance to the wood. This gateway, designed in the style of a Lych* gate, was the gift of Mr John Chadwick, J.P. He presented the Mayoress, Mrs Robert Shorrock, with the key and invited her to unlock the gate and declare the Woods open. The Mayor thanked Mr Chadwick for his gift of the gateway.

Old English Gateway, Sunnyhurst Park, Darwen.

* From the Anglo-Saxon "lytch" meaning corpse. The place where the funeral party used to rest the coffin going into the church

Early 1900

2009

At 4 o'clock the subscribers and dignitaries were invited to a garden party in the Wood, provided by the Mayor, Robert Shorrock.

Borough of Darwen.

Garden Party given by the Mayor and Mayoress (Councillor and Mrs. Robt. Shorrock), to celebrate the Official Opening of the Sunnyhurst Wood, recently acquired by Public Subscription to Commemorate the Coronation of His Majesty King Edward the Seventh.

JULY 2nd, 1903.

Luckily it was a beautiful, sunny day. There was a marquee where light refreshments and musical entertainment were provided.

91

The Deputy Mayor, Alderman Tomlinson, formally presented the deeds conveying the Wood to the Mayor, Mr Shorrock, for the full use and enjoyment of the townspeople of Darwen for ever.

Some of the general public complained that they had not been invited and that the opening day was a Thursday making it difficult for working people to attend. The arrangements went ahead as planned and some people who went to watch the proceedings were invited into the marquee for refreshments.

The stone bridge over the stream leading to the Visitor's Centre and the Kiosk, has the commemorative plaques relating to the opening of the Wood.

2009

2009

2009

93

St Georges Church Consecrated

FIFTY YEARS AGO THE Rev W. A. Duckworth, Lord of the Manor, had promised his brother George who was going to the Crimean War, that if he did not return, a church would be built

in Darwen and named after him. Captain George Duckworth died of cholera at Verna Bay in 1854.

So the Rev Duckworth kept his promise and donated the site and paid for half the cost of

the building. Lower Wood Farm was demolished to make way for the church. Robert Shorrock was one of the local contractors.

On 20th October 1903 the Consecration Service was conducted by Bishop Thornton and the Rev L. Savatard conducted the morning service.

94

Fire at Moss Bridge Mill

ON 29TH OCTOBER 1903 a disastrous fire broke out at Moss Bridge Spinning Mill owned by Messrs C. Shorrock and Co. The mill was fitted with 40,000 spindles and preparation machinery and employed about 150 workers.

Fire broke out in the top room of the building. Sparks fell into a carriage box and were fanned by the draught from the door. Soon there was a sheet of flames and the workers, realising that they could do nothing to extinguish the flames, rushed for safety.

The fire brigade arrived to tackle the blaze and it was soon realised that it was the biggest fire seen in the district for some years. The mill was fitted with sprinklers but these had no effect against such an intense fire.

OTHER EVENTS

J. Rutherford and W. B. Huntington left London on their tour around the world

Further outbreak of smallpox in March

New wing of the Golf Pavilion opened by Mr F. G. Hindle on 16th May

Relief fund opened on 17th October for families of men called to the front in the Boer War and for cotton workers experiencing hard times because of a cotton shortage

Criterion Café opened in November. There was already an old established confectionery business on the premises

1904

IN THIS SECTION

Blackburn Road Wesleyan Chapel opened

Café Chantant started

New museum and art gallery opened

Fish pond in Sunnyhurst Wood constructed

Blackburn Road Wesleyan Chapel Opened

AND HAD BEEN HELD for a considerable time by the Wesleyan Chapel Railway Road Trustees for the building of a school and chapel on Blackburn Road (at the bottom of Bright Street).

A School-Chapel was built in Bright Street and opened by Dr Stephenson on February 16th 1892. The Day School commenced on April 25th 1892 when 30 scholars attended.

The new Chapel was built at a cost of £4616 and opened by the Rev J. Sholl in May 1904. It is now no longer standing and a new Chapel has been built in its place.

It was built of Yorkshire stone and for the windows, lead lights were used throughout. The internal woodwork was pitch pine and the lighting and ventilation were of the latest design. There was a gallery round three sides and the organ chamber and choir chamber were at the back. It could accommodate 650 people. The architect was J. B. Thornley of Darwen and the building contractor was T. Lightbown.

Café Chantant

THIS ACCOUNT WAS TO BE found in the Manchester City News at the beginning of July 1904.

"A bold experiment was made in Darwen on Tuesday and Saturday of last week by the Mayor and Mayoress, Mr. and Mrs. R. Yates. On the outskirts of this prosaic manufacturing town and at the foot of moor land, there is a romantic ravine known as Sunnyhurst Wood which a few years ago was wisely secured by the Corporation for the purposes of a public park. Here it was decided to hold a fete for the benefit of local charities and the entertainment

provided was the Café Chantant, vocal and instrumental music and readings. A proscenium was erected on rising ground among the trees so that a gathering of three to four thousand people were able to witness the performance.

In addition to the play there was a vocal pastorale with rustic dances by children as shepherds, shepherdesses and woodsmen. On Tuesday the weather was not good (it was hastily rearranged in the Co-operative Hall) but Saturday was all that could be desired and the final chorus by some combined choirs numbering two hundred singers was heightened in its effect by the charm of a beautiful summer twilight.

Financially the project was very successful, giving £27 for the Lifeboat Fund and £40 towards providing a days holiday at St. Annes for poor children in the town. Apart however from this practical result too much importance cannot be attached to the

effect which such an afternoon of refined and intellectual recreation will have on the hard working population of a town like Darwen even in years to come.

We understand that some similar performance should be given each year for the benefit of local charities and that possibly a Greek play may be attempted. Great praise is surely due to the Mayoress, as well as to the Mayor, for the boldness and energy which they have displayed in originating and bringing to a successful issue a performance so novel to Darwen and so stimulating in the best sense."

Events of a cultural nature in the small town of Darwen seems to have made a big impression on the citizens of Manchester!

The plays did go on to become an annual event, often giving three performances in a week, in Sunnyhurst Wood if fine and in the Co-operative Hall is wet. James Eccles was involved and he trained the choir and orchestra.

New Museum and Art Galley

ON OCTOBER 26th 1904 the Mayoress, Mrs Ralph Yates, formally opened a new museum and art gallery in the Technical School building. A gold key was presented to her by Alderman Lightbown, and afterwards the party adjourned to the Library.

In the museum there was a small nucleus of birds, shells and stones bequeathed to them by the old library commissioners. Interesting documents and old broadsheets had been lost. The Amateur Photographic Society generously furnished them with a valuable collection of pictures.

Over two hundred people visited the room every evening and many additions were made after the opening.

The entrance to the Museum and Art Gallery on Knott Street.
Today (2010) the building is empty

Fish Pond in Sunnyhurst Wood

AT HIS OWN EXPENSE, Ellis Gibson constructed a fish pond and stocked it with rainbow trout and planted shrubs on its banks. It was finished in December 1904. The pond is at the far end of Sunnyhurst Woods. It measured 115 feet by 37 feet.

Mr. Ellis Gibson

DARWEN people will always have reason to be grateful to Mr. Ellis Gibson, for he was one of a little band that many years ago fought for and obtained the freedom of the Moors. He is the president of the Darwen Angling Society, a capital shot, and one of the keenest of the many sportsmen that are to be found in the district.

It became silted and marshy and recently much effort has been made to bring it back to its original state.

2010

2010

OTHER EVENTS

The Town Council decided to borrow £13,600 for sewage purposes

In September a scheme was adopted for spending £1,200 on new Sewage works

On May 5th, the Mayor, Ralph Yates, was presented with a pair of white gloves at the petty sessional court because there were no cases to be tried (This was the first time for 40 to 50 years)

1905

IN THIS SECTION

The Potter Gateway built

Paddling Pool constructed in Sunnyhurst Wood

The Potter Gateway

JOHN CHARLES POTTER gave £200 for a gateway into Sunnyhurst Wood to be built at the top of Earnsdale Road. It was built as a memento of the many years spent at Earnsdale by himself, his father and other members of the family.

The Potter family established a world famous wallpaper manufacturing business in Darwen starting as C. H. & E. Potter in 1840 at Belgrave Mills and becoming The Wallpaper Manufacturers Limited at the end of the 19th century.

Mr. J. G. Potter, J.P.

They lived at Earnsdale House near the Dingle entrance to the Wood. John Gerald was the son of Charles Potter and entered the business in 1849. He was also active in social work and politics standing as a Liberal candidate in Darwen's first election and just losing to Lord Cranborne. His son, John Charles was educated at Eton and became a barrister. Belgrave Mills was rebuilt in 1896, and the company Wall Paper Manufacturers Limited was formed with John Charles as its chairman.

By permission of Darwen Research Group

The gateway was built in Queen Anne style and was octagonal, measuring 12 feet 6 ins across. Only the road side opening had a gate fitted, the other side was left open. Mr. Smith-Saville was

engaged as the architect with suggestions to design something in keeping

2009

with the sylvan character of the Wood. Originally on the roof of the gateway there was a ball terminal forming the base for a wrought iron vase, having for its crest the Potter crest—a Wyvern. The pointer contained Mr. J. C.

Potter's monogram and was made in copper. The gateway was built by Mr. Baron Harwood in 1905.

The gateway is still there but without the gate and the roof decoration.

Paddling Pool constructed
In Sunnyhurst Wood

ELLIS GIBSON DECIDED TO provide a pond or shallow lake for paddling and sailing model boats. In March this was constructed by the voluntary labour of himself and his friends—Christopher Fish, Robert Preston and Joseph P. Walmsley. The design included three ornamental stone-arched bridges and artificial waterfalls.

In July a fountain on the North side of the pool was built by the same team. This was supplied by a service pond which involved damming a stream higher up the slope so that the fountain, reaching 30 feet in height, could perform in a stone basin. Unfortunately this is no longer there.

On October 2nd 1905 the pond and fountain were formally handed over to the Corporation.

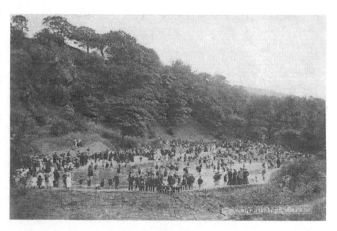

The paddling pool, or wading pool as it was known, was well-used in summer and also in winter if it was frozen for ice skating

The commemorative stone near the pool

2009

OTHER EVENTS

*Floods in Duckworth Street on June 18*th

(The River Darwen burst its banks. This was quite a frequent occurrence)

Cobden Mill opened—see opposite page

The Opening of Cobden Mill

Interesting Celebrations

An interesting party was held at the Millstone Hotel on Friday evening, to celebrate the completion and opening of the new Cobden Mill belonging to Messrs Martin Bros. A large number of officials and overlookers attended, and in addition there were the following gentlemen present: the ex-Mayor (Councillor James Tomlinson), Messrs W., Robert, J. G., A., ad James Martin, Mr Robert Shorrock, J.P., Mr A. Coulthurst (Messrs H. J. and A. Coulthurst), Mr J. R. Jepson (Messrs Willan and Mills), Mr Joseph Hibbert (Messrs Hibbert and Company), and Mr Robert Daltry (Messrs J. M. Daltry and Sons). The catering was as usual, excellent, the high order of previous dinners being again repeated by Mr and Mrs Blackhurst.

Mr J. Walton proposed the toast "The Firm," and said that as co-workers with himself they would hear him out when he said that the friendliness and good feeling exhibited by the firm was a genuine one. (Hear, hear).

Mr T. Jepson added that there was success in store, and if everybody would only pull together as Messrs Martin were trying to pull, the success would come. (Applause).

Mr Robert Martin, in responding, trusted that the good relations which now existed between masters and workmen would continue so. (Hear, hear). Taking advantage of the opportunity, he desired to say that so far as the firm were concerned, they were workmen along with the rest—(hear, hear)—and their only endeavour was to make the conditions for the employees and themselves such that would make it easy for them to procure a big average and big production. The secret of success not only in the cotton trade, but in other businesses as well, was the amount they turned out. (Applause).

Mr H. Whalley submitted the toast "The donors," and expressed the hope that all who had contributed towards the evening's enjoyment would have great success in the future. (Applause). Mr Haythorn also spoke.

Mr J. R. Jepson, in responding said that he had the honour of being present at a similar function to that they were celebrating that evening, when the promoters of the mill held a dinner, along with the contractors, in order to propose the health of the new venture, and bespeak for it a certain amount of success. Nine months ago the revival in the cotton trade had only just commenced, and at that time it was considered a new thing to propose the erection of such an enterprise, but he was glad to see that that revival, had continued throughout the year—(hear, hear)—and he was glad to see that the venture had met with distinct success from the beginning to the end. (Hear, hear). When the promoters began to think about a new mill he remembered at the meeting held for the purpose, that Councillor Tomlinson, the then Mayor, said that their intention was to improve the trade of the town and advance its prosperity. Well, that was a very laudable thing to do on the part of those gentlemen of means in the town—(hear, hear)—and such a worthy aim as that ought to meet with the greatest success. He thought they would be rewarded with success. (Hear, hear). Their intention was not simply the advancement of the town; it was also a means of finding investment of spare capital, and he had no doubt that the venture would prove to the advancement of Darwen and that it would be money well invested. (Hear, hear). They all knew the Martin Bros. as being very honourable business men, and they were deserving of every success. In conclusion, he said he had no doubt that all the men present that evening employed by them would endeavour to make the industry at the lower end of the town a great success. (Applause). Mr Hibbert supplemented the remarks. Mr W. H. Cooper submitted, and Mr James Briggs seconded, "The Trades".

Mr Robert Shorrock, in reply, said he did so with a certain amount of good feeling for all trades carried on in the town. Referring to the cotton trade, he said that as soon as the boom made its appearance there arose a great deal of enthusiasm in the town, and as a result there were today 4,000 extra looms compared with twelve months ago. (Hear, hear). Further, it was a well-known fact that when the cotton trade improved, all the other trades also improved, and he hoped the present conditions would long continue.

The ex-Mayor (Councillor James Tomlinson) endorsed what Mr Shorrock had said. He also pointed out that just after his mayoralty commenced, a number of gentlemen joined the boom in the cotton trade. He had the pleasure of entertaining them in the Mayor's Parlour, and he was glad to know that the most practical results had followed their deliberations. The town recognised the sterling worth of Messrs Martin Bros., and he ventured to think that they all extended to them their good wishes. (Applause).

The Bury quartets party gave selections, and their efforts were augmented by the inimitable Mr Gilligan, a local humorist of considerable repute. Mr A. Crompton, the talented pianist, accompanied.

1906

IN THIS SECTION

Walpamur

Nurses Home moved to new premises

Sundial in Sunnyhurst Wood

Walpamur

THE GREAT COMBINE known as The Wallpaper Manufacturers limited became one of Darwen's leading industries. It began when C. H. and E. Potter took over Belgrave Mill in 1840 and began to produce wallpaper there. The Huntington brothers, experts in design, came from London and Paris to join the Potters as partners in the business.

Belgrave Mill was rebuilt in 1896 without causing any interruption to production and in 1899 the company called The Wallpaper Manufacturers Limited was formed.

Major A. W. Huntington, D.S.O., son of W. B. Huntington became a director of the company. He was instrumental in urging the company to branch out into paint manufacture.

At Hollins Paper Mill, part of the company, an experimental laboratory was set up looking into the possibility of making water paint. On August 2nd 1906 work commenced in a shed at the mill to produce paint which was

The original works staff of eight men and three boys, photographed in 1908.

presented as "Hollins Distemper" and was a success at the Decorators' Exhibition at Leeds. Later it was decided to give the product a more individual name and using the initials of Wall Paper Manufacturers, the name Walpamur was chosen.

In 1915 a private limited company called The Walpamur Company Limited was formed. After the First World War, the company took over Peel and Cobden Mills, to produce water paint.

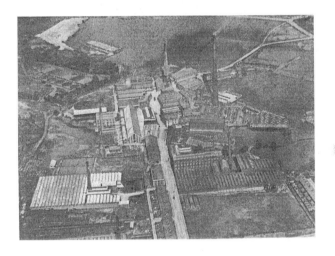

Photographs from Golden Jubilee 1906-1956

On a trademark deigned for Walpamur it shows four prominent landmarks in the town: the spire of St John's Church, Hollins Mill chimney, India Mill chimney and the Jubilee Tower. It was later replaced by just a "W".

The Nurses Home moved to New Premises

ARWEN DISTRICT NURSING ASSOCIATION became the premier charity in the town. It came into being in 1891, chiefly through the interest of Mrs C. P. Huntington (later Lady Huntington) who, when she died in 1911, bequeathed £3,000 to the charity.

The Diamond Jubilee Committee voted £650 of the Jubilee Fund to the Nursing Association on the following terms:

LADY HUNTINGTON.

"That the fund appropriated to the Nursing Association be paid over to two Trustees nominated by the committee of that Association and two Trustees nominated by this committee upon trust to invest the money with the Corporation or upon some other safe security and apply such portion as they think fit but not less than one half of annual income for the purpose of sending patients to Convalescent Hospitals at Southport, Buxton or elsewhere with the aid of the Cotton District Fund and the balance to the General Purposes of the Nursing Association".

The full title of the Association became "Darwen District Nursing Association in Affiliation with Queen Victoria's Jubilee Institute for Nurses".

The chief event of this year, 1906, was the removal of the Nurses Home from Church Terrace, given to the Nursing Association in 1898 by Mr and Mrs C. P. Huntington, to a larger and more convenient house at No. 60 Bolton Road. It was necessary to spend a considerable sum of money in alterations and improvements. The outlay was met by a gift of £200 from Mrs Crook of Stanley Grange, Hoghton.

The Nurses' Home in Bolton Road decorated for the Coronation of King George

The Nurses' Home in Church Terrace

THE DARWEN DISTRICT NURSING ASSOCIATION
(In affiliation with Queen Victoria's Jubilee Institute for Nurses).

Mill and Workshop Collection
FOR THE YEAR 1906.
SATURDAY, DECEMBER 8th, 1906.

The Committee again respectfully solicit your Contributions for the above Association, by making a Collection on its behalf in your Mill or Workshop.

The objects of the Association are " (1) To provide Trained Nurses for the Sick Poor of Darwen in their own homes ; (2) To provide—on Loan—the necessary appliances, &c., required by the Sick."

There are now **four Nurses** for General District Work (in addition to the **two Maternity Nurses** who are doing very good and useful service), instead of three as formerly, and as an additional Nurse involves the Committee in an increased expenditure of nearly £100 a year, they hope that this amount will be made up by the increased Collections of the Workpeople.

From the commencement in 1891 to the end of 1905, the Nurses have attended **5,709** cases, and paid **137,919** visits, and, besides the ordinary cases of sickness, &c., they last year attended in **94** Surgical Operations, **71** cases of Pneumonia, **18** of Cancer, and **31** Accidents, and many others of a serious and tedious nature, the daily visits of the Nurse to one Patient frequently extending over many weeks and sometimes months. (This year's cases and visits are not included).

During the present year the Association have been enabled, from a special fund, to send for three weeks each, 41 Patients to the Southport Convalescent Home, 4 to the Devonshire Hospital, Buxton, and 3 to the Children's Sanatorium, Southport.

The Darwen Medical Society are in full sympathy with the object of the Nursing Association, and two Representatives are on the Management Committee, and they earnestly invite the generous support of the workpeople of Darwen. If desired, the contributions may be paid either to the **General Fund**, to the **Nourishment Fund**, or to the **Special Convalescent Fund**. The Workpeople of any Firm sending a donation of not less than Two Guineas may have the privilege of nominating a representative on the General Committee. The Contributions may be paid by Collectors into the Manchester and County Bank, or to any of the undersigned, and will be thankfully acknowledged.

If the above date is not a convenient one for your Mill, kindly make the Collection as soon as convenient afterwards.

We remain, yours sincerely,

LADY HUNTINGTON, President.

Mrs. WRACK,
Mrs. G. P. HOLDEN, } Vice-Presidents.

Mrs. ECCLES (The Elms), Hon. Secretary.

PERCY C. WINTERTON, Hon. Treasurer.

NATHANIEL JEPSON, Hon. Financial Secretary.

Nurses' Home, 60, Bolton Road,
Darwen, December 1st, 1906.

Dr. GIFFORD, } Representatives from the
Dr. CRAIG, } Medical Society.

WARDLEY & SON, PRINTERS, DARWEN.

This postcard was sold during the First World War to raise funds for the Nursing Association.

Sundial Constructed in Sunnyhurst Wood

IN SUNNYHURST WOOD, near Chadwick Gate, a sundial was constructed in 1906. This was the gift of Mr James Hodkinson of Harwood Street, cotton manufacturer at Lower Wood Mill. Today only the base remains.

THE SUNDIAL, SUNNYHURST WOODS, DARWEN

OTHER EVENTS

Election on January 23rd, J. Rutherford defeated F. G. Hindle by 25 votes

Hoist accident at Belgrave Mills on January 30th. Several men seriously injured

Charles Philip Huntington was created a baronet on June 28th and unfortunately died later in the year

The foundation stone of the new Library was laid on September 22nd by Ralph Yates

Peel Mill constructed (opposite page)

Prospect Mill constructed by John Holden & Sons

Marsh House Mill constructed by Pickup & Company

Darwen's Latest Mill

"Rearing Celebrations"

THE OPENING of a new mill is today not the unusual commercial venture of a few years ago, but it is still a day of considerable moment in the history of any town. It is no passing event, but a venture to be celebrated with all due honours. The opening of the new Peel Mill was celebrated in great festive style on Friday evening last, when some sixty persons sat down to dinner at the Millstone Hotel. The company included the Directors of the Mill Building Company, the tenants of the mill, representatives of the various contractors and the employees upon whom the preparatory work necessary at the starting of a new mill had fallen. The event was of a most enjoyable character. Mr W. H. Blackhurst, the popular host, supplying a first class repast, after which some capital speeches were delivered and an excellent concert took place.

The toast was heartily received, and Mr George Yates, in reply, referred to the local patriotism which characterised the people of Darwen. In their town they had some fine public buildings, a very enterprising municipality, and humanising institutions second to no other industrial town of its size. They rejoiced in the natural advantages of their town, and in this respect he hoped that Corporation would discharge their landscape gardener at Sunnyhurst and leave them their natural sylvan beauties. (Hear, hear). Proceeding to speak of the trade of the town Mr Yates referred of the fact that seven years ago he, as a principal creditor, sold Messrs Bannister their second mill, and now he was proud to be able to state that he was the first to approach them to put before them the advantages of coming to Darwen, and to place them as tenants of one of the finest mills in Lancashire. (Hear, hear). Prior to the Mill Building Company commencing operations a spirit of pessimism passed over Darwen, but since about 4,000 looms had been brought into Darwen and he thought they could claim their share of the advance in the trade in Lancashire. They were also singularly fortunate in Darwen in having a variety of trade, and he thought he was right in saying, without exception, that at the present time they were all paying 10 per cent, and building up some very handsome reserve funds.

In regard to the people of Darwen he doubted whether there were 40,000 people anywhere in the United Kingdom in the aggregate better off financially if they were all clubbed together, and he firmly believed they would go on prospering and their industries would extend. He hoped the Darwen municipality would join Manchester and other municipalities of the country who were going in for more extended bye-laws, to see that the outskirts were laid out to better advantage than our town was. They wanted more open spaces and to relieve the monotony of the streets and idea more of the garden city. (Cheers).

1907

IN THIS SECTION

First Freeman of Darwen

ALDERMAN TIMOTHY LIGHTBOWN, B.A., J.P., was presented with the Honorary Freedom of the Borough of Darwen on January 16th 1907. It is the highest honour it is possible to bestow by any municipality in recognition of long and faithful service. The presentation of this honour was held in the Co-operative Hall to accommodate members of the public.

He occupied many positions during his years of service. These were:

A member of Over Darwen Local Board of Health

A member of the Council from April 1882

Appointed Alderman in April 1888

Chairman of various committees:

Parks and Recreation Grounds

Gas (during reconstruction)

Free Library and Museum

Tramways (during period of initiation)

Electricity

Member of the County Council from its formation in 1889

County Alderman in 1892

Service on County Finance Committee

Member of River Ribble Joint Committee

Justice of the Peace for the Borough 1885

Justice of the Peace for the County 1894

Alderman Eccles, as oldest member of the Council presented him with a silver casket containing a scroll recording Alderman Lightbown's achievements. The casket was obtained from Messrs J. Wood & Sons, Duckworth Street, and was a beautiful example of the silversmith's art.

The casket was on a base of ebony on which there was an inscription, and made of solid silver. On the sides there were enamelled panels, one being the Borough Coat of Arms with a background of Lancashire roses, another being a view of Belgrave Square. On the lid there was the Lightbown crest and motto and his initials T.L. The interior contained the scroll of Freedom and was lined with light blue satin. The scroll was on vellum with ivory handles.

TIMOTHY LIGHTBOWN, ESQ., B.A., C.A.,
HONORARY FREEMAN.

The whole was richly gilded, each separate piece of metal bearing the hallmark, and the delicate moulded work created varying shades producing a truly admirable effect.

This was indeed a great achievement for this son of a handloom weaver, who worked and studied diligently, to receive this high honour.

BOROUGH OF DARWEN.

Presentation of the Honorary Freedom of the Borough

— TO —

Alderman Timothy Lightbown, B.A., J.P.

ORDER OF PROCEEDINGS, 16th JANUARY, 1907.

The Council will assemble on the Platform of the Co-operative Hall at 8 o'clock p.m. prompt.

The Town Clerk will read the Notice convening the Meeting.

The Mayor will request Alderman Eccles and Councillor Yates to conduct Alderman Lightbown on to the Platform.

The Mayor will ask the Town Clerk to read the Resolution of the Council conferring the Honorary Freedom of the Borough upon Alderman Lightbown.

Alderman Eccles will Address the Council in support of the Resolution, and present a Silver Gilt Casket containing a Scroll recording the admission of Alderman Lightbown to be an Honorary Freeman of the Borough.

Alderman Tomlinson and Councillors Yates and Holden will further Address the Council.

The Mayor will then Address the Council, and call upon Alderman Lightbown, who will sign the Roll of Honorary Freemen and afterwards Address the Council.

A Programme of Music will be rendered during the Evening by the following Artistes—

Miss DORA CHENERY, Soprano.
Miss JESSIE YOUNG, Contralto.
Mr. WALTER LAWLESS, Tenor.
Mr. CUTHBERT ALLEN, Baritone.
Mr. ALFRED AINSWORTH, Accompanist.

Strike at Woodside Mill

WOODSIDE MILL WAS ONE of Darwen's larger weaving sheds, started in 1850 by Doctor Graham, Henry Green, Walmsley Preston, Thomas Fish and John Kay. Later Graham Fish ran the mill, retiring in 1899, when The Woodside Mill Company was formed by J. F. Leach and others to run the business. The mill wove mainly for the India and China markets and employed 470 operatives.

In 1907 there was a shortage of yarn because the suppliers of yarn could not keep up with the expansion of the weaving sheds. The yarn was of poor quality and weavers' wages were falling. Some mills had to close for 3½ days but at Woodside Mill there was a strike which lasted just over a year.

A Look at Old Darwen--Lancashire C.C. Library Comm. Darwen Day--Alan Duckworth

126

Falcon Avenue entrance to Sunnyhurst Wood opened

ON WEDNESDAY JUNE 5th 1907 a new entrance to Sunnyhurst Wood at Falcon Avenue was opened by Major A. W. Huntington, D.S.O., (obtained for gallantry in the field in the Boer War).

The photograph shows, left to right, Councillor Worth (Chairman of the Parks Committee), the Mayoress, the Mayor Alderman Ralph Shorrock, Major A. W. Huntington, D.S.O., and Councillor Cooper (Vice-Chairman of the Parks Committee)

He said that he could not claim any personal element in the acquisition of this footpath to the Wood. The land belonged to The Wallpaper Manufacturers Ltd., of which he was a director and a great deal of honour should go to the chairman of the Parks and Recreation Grounds Committee, Councillor Worth.

COUNCILLOR WORTH, J.P.

It was felt that a great number of people came to visit the town and the path would enable them to gain easier access to the Wood. Many difficulties had been overcome by the benefactions of other people: £50 from Mrs T. Lightbown, £50 from Colonel Rutherford, Alderman Eccles gave permission for part of his land to be used.

On opening day the weather was very bad in the earlier part of the day but shortly after noon it began to change and by 3 o'clock it was quite pleasant. Mr Moses Ainsworth and Mr John Beadle promised to provide seats. The Corporation agreed to pay W.P.M. one shilling per year for the right of way from Falcon Avenue to Sunnyhurst Wood.

Everton Street Bowling Club

R. BALLANTYNE WANTED THE Council to provide a Municipal bowling green and it was suggested that an unsightly piece of land next to the Barracks should be used for the purpose. The site had formerly been an old fairground. A lot of volunteers worked on the ground and the Lord of the Manor gave all the sods for the green. The Co-operative Society and Messrs Baldwin undertook all the carting. A cabin was provided by Councillor G. P. Holden.

Everton Street Bowling Green tree planting to commemorate
the Coronation of George V 1911

It was officially opened on Monday July 8th 1907 by the Mayor, Alderman Ralph Shorrock. There was a vote of thanks to the Mayor and to Dr Ballantyne who was President of the Bowling Green and who had

championed the venture. Play was impossible due to an earlier downpour.

Afterwards the company adjourned to the Barracks for refreshments provided by Dr Ballantyne.

It was publicly opened on the Tuesday with a friendly exhibition match in which J. Johnson beat J. Jones. Then a grocers' team beat the Presidents' team 9–4, after which they adjourned to William Street Reform Club for refreshments provided by Mr and Mrs James Jepson.

The bowling green which is circular with the Model Lodging House in the background
(Photograph 2010)

Explosion at Earnsdale Bakery

ON JULY 31st 1907 AT TWELVE noon there was a serious explosion at Earnsdale Bakery owned by Messrs Arthur Shorrock and Son. The explosion came from a heating tube in a steam oven, and was caused by failing to keep the oven in the necessary state of repair. Charles Sayer, a baker, was near the oven and was scalded in the face, causing him to be taken to Blackburn Infirmary.

The explosion had to be investigated and the report indicates that the failure of these tubes in the ovens had become rather frequent of late and would need to be inspected regularly.

Established   1880.

TRY OUR
Sunnyhurst
and other
BISCUITS.

A. SHORROCK & SON,

Wholesale and Retail Bakers and Confectioners,

Agent for
Carr's Malt,
the Ideal -
Brown - -
Bread.

Earnsdale Bakery, 137, Blackburn Road, and Market Hall, Darwen.

AWARDED 70 PRIZES,

INCLUDING THE FOLLOWING—

AWARDED TO A. SHORROCK,

LONDON INTERNATIONAL.

1899—3rd Prize, Medal and Diploma.

1900—V.H. Commended.

1901—2nd Prize, Two Silver Medals and Diploma.

1902—5th Prize (Wheat Meal Bread), Cash and
Diploma.

1904—3rd Prize, Two Bronze Medals and Diploma.

DARWEN, FOR MILK BREAD.

Gold Medal Diploma for HOVIS BREAD,
Manchester, 1903.

Silver Medal and Diploma for Brown Bread,
Newcastle, 1902.

Two Silver Medals, Accrington, 1897.

Silver Medal, Edgworth, 1902.

SCHOOLS, PICNIC PARTIES, and FAMILIES
Supplied on the Shortest Notice.

WEDDINGS and FUNERALS - -
- - - - Catered for.

VAN WILL CALL ON RECEIPT OF POSTCARD.

OFFICIAL COPY

BOILER EXPLOSIONS ACT, 1882 AND 1890

REPORT OF PRELIMINARY INQUIRY

(No. 1706)

EXPLOSION FROM A HEATING TUBE IN A STEAM OVEN AT DARWEN

Cause of the Explosion

The explosion was caused by the failure to keep the oven in the necessary state of repair, working with an undue exposure of the tubes, and a concentration of the chimney draught at one place in the fire, whereby the tube became overheated. Under these conditions the pressure in the tube was rapidly increased and the strength of the iron was reduced until it gave way.

General Remarks

On the date of the explosion a coke fire was lighted in the oven, as usual, about 6 am. About noon, both oven compartments were in full use, with the fire door shut and the damper and ash pit door open. Just then, on hearing an escape of steam, Charles Sayers, a baker, had proceeded from the bench in front of the oven to the fire door, when the explosion took place.

It is stated that both thermometers were showing 450° F, and that the highest temperature used at any time was 500° F, as recommended in the oven builders' instructions, which were posted on the wall of the bakery.

On visiting the premises, I found that the oven had been used during two days after the explosion. The upper half of the burst tube had consequently been burned off 9 inches from the end.

(It goes on from here to described the state of the tubes and why they had "given out")

I am, Sir, Your obedient Servant, J. DOW

Observations of the Engineer Surveyor-in-Chief

This report deals with another failure of a tube in a steam oven at a bakery. The oven had originally contained fifty-three wrought-iron butt welded tubes, the ends of which were hermetically sealed after a small quantity of water had been put into each tube. Each of these tubes therefore was a separate steam vessel.

It would appear that since the oven was first set to work several failures of tubes have occurred, some of the tubes were renewed while five other defective ones were allowed to remain, and, consequently, they were gradually wasted away by the action of the fire, and the explosion is principally attributed to the neglect in not having these tubes renewed, and also in not having the brickwork kept in a proper state of repair, whereby a longer length of tube than the originally intended by the makers was exposed to the heat.

Failures of tubes in appliances similar to this have been rather frequent of late, and the necessity of keeping a close watch for any defects in the tubes or brickwork and having them immediately attended to in order to prevent any loss of life or damage to property, and also ensuring the efficiency of the apparatus, cannot be too strongly brought to the notice of their owners.

PETER SAMSON. The Assistant Secretary, Marine Department, Board of Trade

Drinking Fountain and Gateway
Presented by Mrs T. Lightbown

MRS LIGHTBOWN AND HER husband, Alderman Timothy Lightbown, were great benefactors for the town of Darwen. She generously contributed to the erection of various structures in the parks and countryside of the town, some of which have been vandalised and fallen into disrepair.

Mrs Lightbown was the adopted daughter of Walmsley Preston. She lived at Falcon House with her family and after her marriage to Timothy Lightbown, she and her husband continued to live there. Theirs was a happy marriage but they had no children. This probably accounts for the fact that

they were able to donate a great deal of their fortune to benefit the people of Darwen.

She died in 1909 and her husband died the following year. In 1907, she provided funds for the erection of a gateway in Whitehall Park and for a drinking fountain in Sunnyhurst Wood.

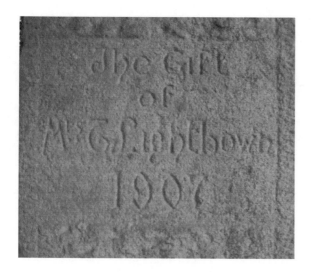

The inscription on the gateway

The Lightbown Gateway in Whitehall Park

The inscription on the fountain

The Drinking Fountain in Sunnyhurst Wood

134

Hollins Grove Chapel

IN 1905 IT WAS DECIDED to build a new Chapel and convert the present building for use as a Day and Sunday school. By December 1905, the promises to the "New Chapel Building Fund" had amounted to £1,632, and at the end of 1906 the amount was over £3,087. Alderman and Mrs Eccles were great

benefactors to the Chapel. He gave £1,000 when the fund was first launched and Mrs Eccles gave £1,000 when she laid the foundation stone. They pledged to give £1 for every £1 raised.

On February 23rd 1907, the foundation stone was laid by Mrs A. T. Eccles. In June of this year the Reverend J. W. Coulton began his ministry. The new chapel was opened on December 12th by Miss Eccles, daughter of Alderman A. T. Eccles.

The chapel had been provided with an excellent, almost new organ and would accommodate 750 people. At the opening service there were five eminent preachers. The building fund stood at £6,115 at the end of 1907.

Not only had a new chapel been built and a new organ installed but alterations had been made to the old Chapel buildings so that they could be used as a day school. These were completed and opened on December 7th 1908 by Mrs A. T. Eccles. The school provided accommodation for 518 scholars. The cost of the complete scheme was £9,118.

Photograph of the old Chapel which became a School

OTHER EVENTS

The Marquis of Salisbury visited on April 30th

Severe thunderstorm in May

Snowstorm in July

Silver Jubilee of St Edwards Church on August 18th

Disastrous fire at Coulthurst's Robert Street Foundry on
September 5th (Damage £2,000 to £3,000)

D. J. Shackleton elected Chairman of the Parliamentary
Committee of the Trade Union Congress on September 7th

Mr D. J. Shackleton, M.P.

Victoria Street

1908

IN THIS SECTION

The New Free Library Opened

IN 1904 DARWEN LIBRARY COMMITTEE applied to Mr Andrew Carnegie, American philanthropist originally from Scotland, for money to build a new library. He gave the sum of £8,000. At this time the library was housed in the Technical School but more space was needed for the school, so a new library needed to be built.

ANDREW CARNEGIE, ESQ., D.L.,
HONORARY FREEMAN.

Ralph Yates laid the foundation stone in September 1906

It was found that £8,000 was not sufficient to cover the costs, so Mr Ralph Yates went to visit Mr Carnegie in Scotland. After discussions Mr Carnegie raised the sum to £10,000 but made the condition that this would include a Juvenile Room instead of the Museum and Art Gallery.

The contractor appointed was Mr Robert Shorrock and work began in March 1906. In September of that year, Ralph Yates laid the foundation stone.

The building was completed early in February 1908 and opened for business on February 24th. It was officially opened by Mr Carnegie who arrived in Darwen by train at three o'clock on Wednesday May 27th. The Mayor, G. P. Holden, welcomed the guests and invited Ralph Yates to present the souvenir key to Mr Carnegie who addressed the company, unlocked the door and entered the building. Later, in the lecture hall, the honour of the Freedom of the Borough was conferred upon Mr Carnegie and he was presented with the associated scroll and casket. He left at 5-18 pm.

Plaque in the entrance hall

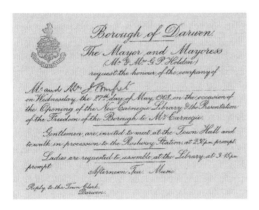

2010

Over the library door

141

Fire at India Mill

ON JUNE 15th 1908 AT ABOUT 9 o'clock in the morning, there was a loud explosion in Darwen Paper Mill next to India Mill. It came from a boiler which was used for pumping purposes and weighed 8 cwt. A short time later there was steam coming from the 6th storey of India Mill and there, 130 feet above ground level, was the missing boiler! It seems it had crashed through the roof of India Mill on to a spinning mule, much to the surprise of all concerned. The man in charge of the boiler was badly scalded and bruised but luckily not more seriously hurt and no one else was injured. Later, when the hole was being repaired, the tar being used for this purpose caught fire. There was a lot of smoke but luckily the fire did not cause too much damage.

General Booth Visited

ON JULY 8th 1908 GENERAL BOOTH, the founder of the Salvation Army, visited Darwen. This well-respected, popular gentleman was given a wonderful welcome and was publicly received by the Mayor, G. P. Holden. Later General Booth went to the Co-operative Hall to speak on "The Salvation Army—Past, Present and Future."

He travelled along Blackburn Road to arrive in Darwen at 10-15 am and left shortly after 2 o'clock, going down Church Street and up Bolton Road.

Photograph by permission of Darwen Research Group

St Cuthbert's Church Bell Tower

ON MONDAY SEPTEMBER 21st 1908, Mrs J. W. Gillibrand formally opened the bell tower of St Cuthbert's Church. The excavations for the foundations of the tower began in May last

year, 1907 and the foundation stone was laid by Mrs Gillibrand on August 31st. The first part of the church, built in 1875, cost over £8,000 and the cost of this extension amounted to over £6,000.

In the evening at 7-30 pm there was a dedication service in which the Bishop of Manchester, Dr Knox, was the central figure and was received at the church by the vicar, Rev J. Forbes, M.A.

The architect was Mr R. W. Smith-Saville who was a church warden and gave his services free. The clock was added later in 1916.

Baptist Chapel Jubilee

THE BAPTIST CAUSE IN Darwen was formed in 1858 in William Street School. William Snape, Darwen's first Mayor, was one of the pioneers of the Baptist movement in Darwen and one of the first Superintendents of the Sunday School. The Baptist Chapel in Bolton Road was opened on November 27th 1862 at a cost of £3,000.

For the Jubilee celebrations, in 1908 the Chapel was repaired and renovated at a cost of over £150. The re-opening services were conducted on October 11th by the pastor, the Rev John W. Walker. At the close of morning service, 8 people received the rite of

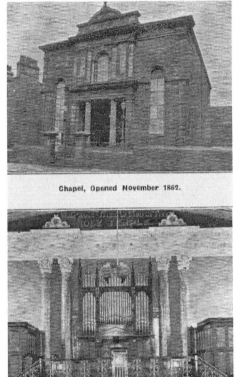

Chapel, Opened November 1862.

Organ, Opened August, 1896.

baptism and were welcomed into the fellowship of the Chapel at the evening service. The celebrations included a Musical Service and reached a climax on October 25th with the visit of Dr J. T. Marshall, M.A., President-elect of the Baptist Union.

2010

Falcon Avenue Gateway Presented

THE PREVIOUS YEAR THE NEW entrance to Sunnyhurst Wood at Falcon Avenue had been opened. Mrs Johnson-Grime, wife of George Johnson-Grime of Church Terrace, expressed a wish to present a gateway for this new entrance. It was designed in a Chinese-style with woodwork of solid oak and red tiles on the roof. There were oak railings on either side in the same design, completing the structure. It was opened in 1908.

This gateway fell into disrepair and in 1957 was replaced by a new one with stone pillars and metal gates and railings. Recently (2009/2010) it has been repainted and renovated and a plaque has been placed on the gatepost.

Entrance, Sunnyhurst Wood, Darwen

Theatre Royal

IN 1908 MR WILL DALTON, variety agent, took over the Theatre Royal in Railway Road and changed the name to the "Hippodrome", showing animated films and variety performances. In this year on April 3rd, Winston Churchill addressed a big Liberal meeting there on the subject of "Free Trade and the Licensing Bill".

Originally, in 1877, this building was intended to be a Temperance Hall but was soon converted into a theatre, the Theatre Royal.

In about 1880, Mr J. W. Riley became the lessee and formed a repertory company with the leading lady being Miss Ellen Beaufort. Mr J. R. Horrocks became a very successful manager and painted all the scenery. In 1881 there was an amateur performance of "The Queen's Shilling" with Mr F. G. Hindle and Major W. H. Place being members of the cast. Mr W. B. Huntington's family and friends were responsible for many productions. Usually at Christmas there was a pantomime, the first ones being Robinson Crusoe and Jack the Giant Killer.

Many famous artists are said to have performed there: Dan Leno, Vesta Tilley, Lily Langtry, Charlie Chaplin and Houdini.

THEATRE ROYAL
DARWEN.

FOR POSITIVELY SIX NIGHTS ONLY, COMMENCING

Monday, Jany. 26th, 1903,

ALSO ONE DAY PERFORMANCE ON

SATURDAY AFTERNOON, JANY. 31ST, AT 2 O'CLOCK.

— MR. JOHN WALTER'S —

HAS THE HONOUR TO ANNOUNCE THAT HIS ENTIRE PANTOMIME COMPANY FROM THE
ST. JAMES' THEATRE, MANCHESTER, WILL APPEAR IN

"Robinson Crusoe"

WRITTEN BY MR. ALFRED RUTLEY.

POURTRAYED by the MOST POWERFUL CO. of ARTISTES TOURING in the PROVINCES To-day,—
Including,—

Miss Constance St. Bride.

Miss Winnie Scott,	Miss Marie Winsome,
Miss Emilie Liske,	Miss Connie Arden,
Miss Gerty Wasley,	Miss Mill May,

Mr. Fred Alberto,

Mr. Will Saunders,	Mr. Leo Lester,
The Brothers Daniels,	The Brothers Renz,

The Four Laureens,

Mr. Bert Pearson,	Mr. Charlie Arnett,

AND

The Brothers Obo,

SUPPORTED BY

A Full and Powerful Chorus, Ballet and Auxiliaries.

SUPERB SCENERY by T. E. RYAN, BERNARD WHITE, W. COLEMAN and R. W. MILLER.
RICH and COSTLY DRESSES.   ALL THE LATEST SONGS and DANCES

THE PANTOMIME STAGE MANAGED AND ARRANGED BY MR. BERT ALBERT, AND PRODUCED UNDER THE
PERSONAL SUPERVISION OF MR. AND MRS. JOHN WALTERS.

Business Manager ... ... Mr. LOUIS J. BEARD.

OTHER EVENTS

Presentation of the Primrose League Order of the Grand
Star to Mrs J. H. Wraith on February 18th

Gymnastic Club formed on March 2nd

The Mayor opened a distress fund on October 29th

Councillor G. P. Holden, J.P., presented a 65 horse power
motor car to the Corporation for special use by the Fire
Brigade on November 10th

1909

IN THIS SECTION

First Darwen Scout Group

Roller Skating

First Darwen Scout Group

IN 1907 ROBERT BADEN POWELL started the Scout Movement and the following year wrote "Scouting for Boys". This inspired boys from Duckworth Street and Belgrave Churches to form a

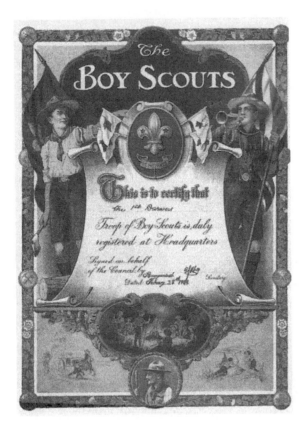

patrol called the "Curlews" and this was registered in February 1908, and based at Belgrave. A smaller group formed a patrol at Duckworth Street.

Eventually the two groups at Belgrave and Duckworth Street joined forces and on February 28th 1909 the combined group was registered officially as the 1st Darwen Troop.

A photograph of the Group taken in 1913

Roller Skating

THE CRAZE FOR ROLLER SKATING arrived in Darwen in 1909 and started to become less popular in 1911. Robert Shorrock, the Darwen contractor, had erected a skating rink in Manchester. In Darwen there were two at first: The Victoria at Livesey Fold and The Swiss at Hollins Grove, which was at the Conservative Club where the Assembly Rooms were utilised as a rink and a maple floor was placed over the existing one, the cost of which was met out of the profits.

The Imperial Skating Rink at Cotton Hall

On June 5th the Building Committee passed plans for:

1. A skating rink in Grimshaw Street for the Empress Skating Company Limited

2. An extension to the skating rink at Livesey Fold for the Victoria Skating Company Limited

3. A skating rink at Cotton Hall for the Imperial Rink Company. The Cotton Hall Skating Rink covered an area of 10,000 sq.ft. (three times the size of the Co-operative Hall) and had a roof span of 81 ft. The contractor was Mr Robert Shorrock and the architect was Mr John B. Thornley. This was the most popular of the skating rinks. It had accommodation for over 2,000 and large crowds of over 1,000 often watched rink hockey matches there. The rinks had to have a licence and usually had three sessions daily and closed at 10 pm.

OTHER EVENTS

Chapels Conservative Club was opened by John Rutherford,

M.P., on September 4th

Whitehall Bowling Club opened

Sunnyhurst Bowling Club opened

1910

IN THIS SECTION

Bull Hill Hospital opened new building

Darwen Industrial Co-operative Society Jubilee

Sudell Road School opened

Bull Hill Hospital Opened
New building

A NEW TYPHOID FEVER hospital was opened on Thursday April 14th 1910 in the grounds of the old hospital but distinctly separate. It had eight beds and was entirely for typhoid fever cases leaving the old hospital to accommodate other fevers and infectious diseases. The cost of the building was £2,000 but it was necessary in order to save taking patients to the Blackburn Union Hospital which had caused expense and problems.

Darwen Industrial Co-operative Society Jubilee

CO-OPERATION IN DARWEN began in 1860. After a meeting held in Ramsden's Temperance Hotel in Railway Road, a shop was acquired in Green Street. This was a success and a second shop was opened in Bolton Road. Other shops were opened during the "Cotton Famine" when times were very hard. Amazingly in spite of difficult economic circumstances it was decided to build some central premises in

School Street and in 1866, Thomas Hughes (author of Tom Brown's Schooldays) laid the foundation stone. The premises were officially opened in 1868.

During this time (1900-1914) several new branches were opened:

Cemetery Road	1900
Anchor	1901
Barley Bank	1906
Sunnyhurst	1912
Two Gates	

Spring Bank, Heys Lane and Wood Street were given new premises.

To celebrate 50 years of the Society's existence, several events were arranged.

A C.W.S. exhibition

An employees' party and picnic

An old people's tea party and concert

A children's gala and entertainment

Distribution of 3,000 copies of the souvenir handbook

The children's entertainment was in the Cotton Hall Skating rink in October with 1,500 children present. There were silent films (Charlie Chaplin and Wild Westerns), a blind concertina player, singers and conjurers. The children were presented with an apple and an orange, a commemorative mug and a linen handkerchief with the Society's central premises on it.

In August 1989 a spectacular fire swept through the partially demolished School Street premises.

There was an annual Co-op Gala held on the Anchor Ground

These photographs are probably of
the Jubilee Gala

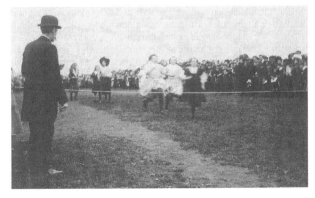

Sudell Road School Opened

SUDELL ROAD SCHOOL WAS the first Lancashire County Council School built in Darwen and there is an inscription on the front of the building stating this. It was opened on December 29th 1910 and was an undenominational school, taking in both boys and girls from seven years up to leaving age which was thirteen years.

It was a one storey building of local stone with large, high windows, and considered a big improvement on other schools in the town. The teachers did not specialise but taught all subjects to their class. The school hall was used for Physical Training and swimming

The inscription says First Council School

instruction was given at the Peel Baths. The Anchor Ground was used for football and for the Town's School Sports where Sudell Road usually won the "Tug-of-war" competition.

When they were twelve years of age, all pupils became half-time, working in the cotton mills and doing spare-time jobs as well as being at

school. This half-time system was abolished in 1918.

Today Sudell Road is a Primary School, but had previously been a Secondary Modern School.

162

OTHER EVENTS

F. G. Hindle became Member of Parliament for Darwen on January 25th

with a majority of 211 over J. Rutherford. In December

.J. Rutherford regained his seat

Death of Edward VII on May 6th

Proclamation of George as King at the Circus on

May 9th

Funeral and Memorial Service on May 20th

Labour Exchange opened in Bridge Street on

July 23rd

Alderman Lightbown died on September 7th and

bequeathed £10,000 for Educational, charitable

and municipal purposes in the town

Centenary of the Oddfellows on September 24th

They held meetings in Eccles Rooms, Market Street

D. J. Shackleton appointed senior Labour adviser at the Home Office on

November 11th

HOLY TRINITY CHURCH,
DARWEN.

King Edward VII.

MEMORIAL
SERVICE.

20th MAY, 1910.

Offertory for the Whitehaven Colliers' Fund.

1911

IN THIS SECTION

Sundial in Whitehall Park

MRS WALMSLEY PRESENTED a Sundial to Whitehall Park in memory of her husband Councillor William Walmsley, who had been Chairman of the Parks Committee.

Councillor Walmsley was the owner of Industry Mill and they lived at Cornfield Cliff. Mrs Walmsley presented the Sundial on May 27th 1911 and died soon afterwards in July.

2009

Today the sundial is in a state of disrepair and the plaque is difficult to read.

Coronation of George V

ON THE DAY OF THE Coronation, June 22nd 1911, special services were held in most churches. Many buildings in the town were decorated with flags and bunting and there were 3,000 burners on the Municipal buildings.

The later part of the morning was occupied by a large procession assembling in the Market Square then travelling through the main streets and returning to the Market Square. The Mayor, Councillor W. P. Kay, read a proclamation of the King's Coronation and then hymns were sung. In the afternoon a great gathering of school children occupied the Square and they were given medals and Coronation mugs. On the following day the children were entertained with galas at Turncroft and at the Anchor field.

Local brass bands played in the parks and in the Market Square; these were The Pickup Bank Band, The Salvation Army Band and The Darwen Borough Band. There was a fountain in the Market Square and a bonfire was lit on the moors.

A new gateway was built at Whitehall Park to commemorate the Coronation and the daughter of the Mayor, Miss Alice Kay, planted an oak tree. In Bold Venture Park, there was a display of flowers making the picture of the royal crown and the aviary had been replenished with 70 birds and also a few lizards, tortoises, Greentree frogs and a snake. In the evening there were illuminations in Sunnyhurst Wood.

The celebrations started on the Thursday and went on until Saturday evening.

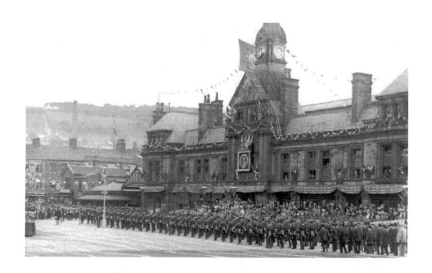

Darwen News Office

Hargreaves in Railway Road

Angel Inn at the Circus

A decorated tram going down
Bolton Road to the Circus

Whitehall Park Gates

FROM 1908-1911 WHEN many people were out of work, the Council decided to have the bottom part of Whitehall Park dug out and landscaped, thus providing employment for a number of these people. At the entrance to this part of the Park some splendid gates were erected.

At 5-30pm on Coronation Day these new gates

were formally opened by the Mayor, W. P. Kay. Councillor Worth, Chairman of the Parks Committee, presented the Mayor with a souvenir key.

National Rail Strike

FROM AUGUST 17th TO 20th 1911 there was a national Rail Strike. On August 18th, employees at Darwen Station from the Goods and Passenger Departments came out in sympathy. These were men connected with the Amalgamated Society of Railway Servants, the General Railway Workers Union and the Signalmen and Pointsmens Union. The men affected at Darwen were:

 10 Passenger porters

 35 Goods porters

 3 Van men

 15 Signal men

 9 Plate layers

And at Spring Vale:

 4 Passenger porters

 15 Goods porters

 9 Signal men

 5 Plate layers

The only officials remaining at Darwen were Mr Higginbottom, the Station Master and Mr Dearnley, the Chief Clerk who had to undertake porters' duties and collecting tickets.

Consecration of St Barnabas Church

THE MISSION CHURCH which had been used for Divine Service since 1884 was consecrated on December 8th 1910 by Bishop Knox and on January 23rd 1911, St Barnabas Church separated from the Mother Parish of St John's.

At the Consecration Service the party proceeded up the nave to the communion table singing the 24th psalm. The Chancellor read aloud the Sentence of Consecration which the Bishop signed. The Bishop then delivered a short sermon.

2010

OTHER EVENTS

Fire at Hollins Grove Paper Mill on February 18th

Fire at Lower Darwen Paper Mill on May 15th

Darwen Literary Society Commemoration Dinner of 30th Session

First Annual Dog Show on November 18th

Lady Betty Balfour came to the town and spoke on Women's Suffrage on November 28th

DARWEN LITERARY SOCIETY.

March 5th. 1912.

Dear Sir,

The Committee have decided to commemorate the close of the 30th Session of the Society by holding a Conversazione and Social Evening in the Library Rooms, on Thursday, the 14th inst. This is the day following the opening of the Exhibition of Pictures which is being arranged by Mr. George Yates, J.P. and the Free Library Committee, and all the Exhibits will be on view for the Conversazione.

A Miscellaneous Programme of Music and Recitals is being arranged, and the Committee hope that by the presence of yourself and friends you will assist in making the event a successful one and fully worthy of the occasion.

TICKETS (price 2/6 including refreshments) are now ready and may be had from any Member of the Committee or from the undersigned.

Yours truly,

R. H. BALDWIN, President.

The black and white sketch on the cover of the Programme was the work of J. H. Morton

172

1912

IN THIS SECTION

Exhibition of Paintings

MR GEORGE YATES OF WOODLANDS, organised and financed an exhibition of paintings in the Library opening on Wednesday March 13th 1912. The paintings were displayed in the Lecture Hall where the artificial lighting had been greatly improved. There were 170 pictures in the collection, which were insured for £30,000. It was hoped that it would create a desire to establish a permanent art gallery in the town.

Mr Yates went to a great deal of trouble to secure a variety of paintings loaned from both public and private owners. There was a drawing by Turner, a water colour by John Ruskin and a pastel by J. H. Morton (of Darwen). Mr Yates, himself provided 11 paintings for the exhibition.

The exhibition was opened by Councillor Butterworth of Manchester. Mr J. Rutherford, M.P., and Mr J. W. Marsden spoke on behalf of those who had loaned pictures. A vote of thanks to Councillor Butterworth was proposed by Ralph Yates and Councillor W. P. Kay. The company were afterwards entertained to light refreshments by Mr and Mrs George Yates.

The exhibition closed at 8-30pm on April 3rd and had been attended by about 15,000 people.

Sunnyhurst Wood Tea Room Opened

TO CELEBRATE THE CORONATION of George V it was decided to build a tea house in Sunnyhurst Wood. The architect endeavoured to make it a typically old English building, Elizabethan in style and at first it was known as the Old English Tea

G. R.

BOROUGH OF DARWEN.

Official Opening by the Mayor (Councillor John Pickup, J.P.) of the Tea House (in Sunnyhurst Wood), recently erected by Public Subscription to Commemorate the Coronation of His Majesty King George the Fifth. :: :: ::

16TH MAY, 1912.

House. The funds for its construction were raised by public subscriptions and of the £1,500 subscribed; donations of £450 each were made to Darwen Nursing Association and East Lancashire Infirmary.

There were two stained glass windows in one of the front bays, one showing the Borough Arms and the other the Royal Arms, and on the opposite wall a statuette of Queen

Elizabeth I, which was a gift of Messrs Shaw and Co., of Waterside. These can still be seen today.

The quaint stone lintel to the front door had formed a kitchen fireplace in one of the old cottages which had been demolished. Some of the old oak beams from these cottages were used in the porch and some were used in the open timbered roof of the Tea House.

The official opening was on May 16ᵗʰ 1912 when the Mayor, John Pickup, J.P., and his party assembled in the Tea House grounds at 3·00pm. There is a commemorative plaque on the wall.

This is a programme of the events:

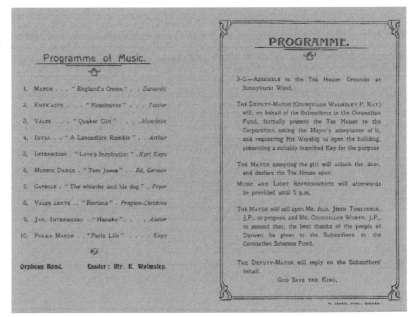

Presentation of Greenway Shelter

ON HIS COMING OF AGE, Mr Charles Spencer Greenway presented the gift of a shelter to Sunnyhurst Wood, on August 10th 1912. It was built in the style of an old country-town market

shelter and its purpose was to give the maximum amount of protection in the event of a sudden shower and at the same

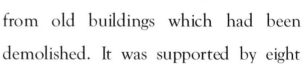

time keeping everything as open as possible. The roof

was covered with stone slates which had been collected from old buildings which had been demolished. It was supported by eight

stone pillars and on one of these there was an inscription.

Charles Spencer Greenway was the grandson of the Rev. Charles Greenway. Unfortunately, in 1916 he died of scarlet fever when working for the British Embassy in Petrograd.

The shelter was used for the popular Café Chantant entertainments.

Charles Spencer Greenway

Earnsdale Cotton Waste Mill Fire

ON MONDAY AFTERNOON, September 30th 1912 smoke was seen coming from the top storey of the yarn warehouse of Messrs Henry Yates and Son, Earnsdale Mill. It was a four storey building and the outbreak occurred in the willow waste room.

The fire soon spread through the rest of the building which had been recently equipped with some splendid new machinery. Some of the workmen tried to extinguish the flames with a hose-pipe but they were unsuccessful and had to make a hasty retreat from the building. They realised that one of their fellow workers was missing and they tried to search for him but were beaten back by the dense smoke.

The fire brigade soon arrived on the scene with sixteen men, the engine and other appliances. A plentiful supply of water was obtained from the mill lodge, but their efforts had little effect on the burning building. The Belgrave Mill brigade arrived on the scene to assist with the fire and to stop the flames spreading to other premises and to the offices and in this the brigades were successful. In the evening the Hoddlesden brigade were sent for to provide some relief. Eventually the fire burnt low but the mill was in ruins with only four walls left standing. The police had to control large crowds who had assembled to watch.

When the fire brigade were able to search through the smouldering ruins they found the charred body of Herbert Gregory who was an engineer and had been trying to put out the fire with the other workmen. Later another body was found in the debris and was believed to be Henry Riley.

Mr Ralph Yates expressed the grief of his firm at the loss of life which had attended this unfortunate fire.

The Huntington Bridge Opened

ON SATURDAY NOVEMBER 9th 1912 Major Arthur Huntington, D.S.O., opened the Huntington Bridge in Sunnyhurst Wood. The bridge was built in commemoration of his father, William Balle Huntington, D.L., J.P., with funds donated by the employees of Belgrave and Hollins paper mills. Mr Huntington died in 1911 and left money in his will for his employees to be paid

before Christmas, not waiting for probate. He left:

> 1 days pay for under 5 years service
>
> 1 weeks pay for 5-10 years service
>
> 2 weeks pay for 10-15 years service
>
> 3 weeks pay for 15-20 years service
>
> 4 weeks pay for over 20 year's service

In certain cases he left shares to managers, foremen and staff.

On the day of the opening the weather was fine and up until the opening ceremony workmen had been busily employed putting the finishing touches to the work. By the time people arrived they had tidied away their tools and put a cord across the entrance. The bridge was an imposing stone structure replacing planks by which the stream was originally crossed. The letter "H" was incorporated in the design on the parapets. The bridge was constructed by Mr Thomas Lightbown and designed by Mr Smith-Saville.

View from the bridge towards the paddling pool

Demonstration by Gustav Hamel

USTAV HAMEL, A FAMOUS AVIATOR, brought his Bleriot monoplane by train to Darwen for a demonstration on the Anchor Ground on Saturday November 16th 1912. He was 23 years of age.

The Darwen News reported that: "The machine has a strong resemblance to a huge kite and one is struck by the delicacy of its make, lightness, of course, being essential to successful aviation." The paper expressed the hope that the people of Darwen would avail themselves of this unique opportunity to witness a flight as it was unlikely

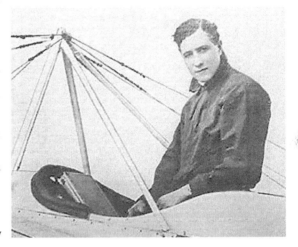

that this would occur again for some considerable time. Unfortunately the

attendance was not as large as anticipated. The gate receipts amounted to £75 showing that less than 3,000 had paid for admission to the ground. Hamel's contract was for 55 per cent of the total takings.

The Darwen News reported that: "Saturday was a most suitable day in every respect for Hamel to give an exhibition, scarcely any wind interfering with the flights. It was shortly before half past two that preparations were made for the first flight, when the airman's engineers brought the Bleriot monoplane from the temporarily erected aerodrome. Taking his seat, the famous aviator soared into the air and made a series of circuitous flights at an altitude of about 100 feet, occasionally descending in bird-like fashion and causing some anxious moments among a portion of the crowd by guiding the monoplane just above their heads. At times he gave the impression that he would collide with the onlookers and drop in the midst of them, until the wonderful control Mr Hamel had over his machine was realised. He alighted on the playing pitch to the ringing cheers of the spectators. In his circuitous trips, Hamel covered an area stretching from Moss Bridge to Sunnyhurst on the one hand and the Heights and the Ironworks on the other and at one period he must have been 1,000-2,000 feet from terra firma."

His plane arriving at Windsor Castle

Gustav Hamel was an Englishman of German extraction and the son of the Royal Physician. He learnt to fly at the Bleriot School in France when he was 21 years of age. To mark the Coronation of King George V, he flew his aeroplane 21 miles between Hendon and Windsor on September 9th 1911, carrying letters and postcards. For this he was credited with flying the world's first airmail service. He had crossed the Channel 11 times and had covered the journey from London to Paris in one day and from Paris to London in another. He was planning a transatlantic attempt when unfortunately he went missing on a cross-Channel flight from Paris in 1914.

OTHER EVENTS

Lady Huntington left £3,000 in trust for the Nursing Association on January 6ᵗʰ

The miners come out on strike for the minimum wage on January 12ᵗʰ

New Salvation Army premises were opened in Wood Street on September 14ᵗʰ. Councillor G. P. Holden gave £100 towards new premises. (Became Wardleys (printers), then Gibsons)

The Town Council decided to adopt a by-law enforcing all vehicles to have rear lights on October 7ᵗʰ

New warehouse in Borough Road opened by the Industrial Co-operative Society on October 10ᵗʰ

Moss Bridge Weaving Mill constructed by Darwen Mill Building Co., Ltd

Premier Mill constructed by the same Company

1913

IN THIS SECTION

Darwen Jockey's Narrow Escape At Ascot

ALBERT "SNOWY" WHALLEY was born in Darwen in 1885. His father had a barber's shop near the White Lion on the Green. When he was 13 years of age he ran away from home to try to find work in the stables at Newmarket, headquarters of horse racing. He worked hard for 7 years without managing to ride in a race. When his master retired, instead of returning home, he decided to try his luck in India. There he was a success and was champion jockey several times. In 1910 he returned to England and rode for some of the top owners, having  23 winners in the first season and 29 in the next. He was third in the Jockeys' Championship.

In 1913, in the Derby, he narrowly avoided hitting the suffragette, Emily Davidson, who ran out in front of the King's horse. Again, a fortnight later, he was riding in the Ascot Gold Cup when a man ran in front of him waving a pistol and shouting "Stop". This, of course, proved impossible to do. In this year he rode 86 winners.

After the First World War, in 1919, he won his first classic, the 1,000 Guineas and the following year won The Oaks. He retired from racing in 1924.

The Royal Visit of
King George and Queen Mary

ON JULY 10th 1913 King George and Queen Mary paid an official visit to Darwen as part of their tour of Lancashire. This was the first visit of a reigning monarch to the town and unfortunately was of short duration (about 30 minutes), but was a red letter day for

Darwen. In the Market Square a grandstand with a large reception platform had been erected decorated with flags and flowers.

The King and Queen with Lord Derby, their host, travelled from Blackburn by motor car and arrived in the Market Square to be greeted by the Mayor, Mr F. Hindle and the Mayoress, his mother, Mrs F. G. Hindle. At 3-40pm slightly later than expected, the gun on the top of the Market

hall had announced that the royal car had entered the Borough at Earcroft. Holy Trinity bells started ringing and there was a huge cheer from about 8,000 school children. The Mayor's fiancée, Miss Lawrence was presented to the King and Queen, who expressed good wishes for their future together. Also on the platform with the Mayor and Mayoress were Councillor and Mrs John Pickup (ex-Mayor), Alderman and Mrs Eccles, Alderman and Mrs Cocker, the Coronation Mayor and Mayoress (Mr and Mrs W. P. Kay) and Colonel John Rutherford, M.P.

Territorials, Reserves, Police, Fire Brigade etc were all massed in the Square and old people were accommodated in a special stand. School children sang the National Anthem, and then several people were presented to the King and Queen.

The Royal Party then travelled up Bolton Road to the entrance of Whitehall Park where they would see the gates erected to commemorate their Coronation.

When the King and Queen had left the Market Square, the Mayor and Mayoress went to Sunnyhurst Wood to plant an oak tree to commemorate the visit.

THE MAYOR AND MAYORESS OF DARWEN
(MR. F. HINDLE JR. AND MRS. F. G. HINDLE)
request the honour of the company of

Mr & Mrs J. Pomfret

on Thursday, July 10th, 1913, at the Tea House,
Sunnyhurst Wood, Darwen, on the
occasion of the Planting of an Oak Tree in Commemoration of
the Visit of Their Majesties to Darwen.

Afternoon Tea, 4-15.   R.S.V.P.
Tree Planting Ceremony, 5-15.   Mayor's Parlour,
                                        Darwen.

BOROUGH OF
DARWEN

VISIT
OF
Their Majesties
King George V.
AND
Queen Mary,
JULY 10th 1913.
Souvenir of the Royal Visit.

Facsimile of the Frontispiece to the Souvenir presented
to their Majesties the King and Queen.

OTHER EVENTS

Lord Salisbury came and addressed a big Primrose League demonstration on February 21st

A scheme was initiated for taking over Bull Hill Fever Hospital as a Sanatorium for consumptive patients on March 18th

The Dingle Bowling Green was presented by Mr J. C. Potter on August 1st

A new fire station in Charles Street was opened on August 7th

Southend Mill constructed by the Albert Spinning Co., Ltd

Sunnyhurst Mill constructed by the Sunnyhurst Mill Co., Ltd

1914

IN THIS SECTION

Olympia Picture Palace opened

New Garden Village built

Spring Bank School opened

Jubilee of St John's Church

Moss Bridge Hospital

Olympia Picture Palace opened

THE PROPRIETOR OF THE OLYMPIA was Mr Harry Yorke and he opened his "Palatial Place of Entertainment" on Monday March 2nd 1914. There was nothing in the way of formality in the opening.

The entertainment was announced to commence at 2-45pm on Monday afternoon and for fully an hour before that, people thronged round the door clamouring for admission. When the first picture was on the screen, nearly every one of the 1,200 seats was occupied and those present included

The Olympia cinema was demolished to make way for Hardman Way

the families of many professional and other gentlemen in the town.

Courteous door-keepers passed visitors from their cars to the neatly dressed lady attendants in their black dresses and white muslin aprons, who conducted them to comfortable seats.

Later on these dainty maidens brought round a tray with tea, sugar and biscuits to each individual except those in the very cheapest seats. It made one marvel at the astonishing amount of enjoyment one can have for sixpence. The main film was called "The Bishop's Carriage".

THE OLYMPIA, DARWEN.

Proprietor and Manager : Mr. HARRY YORKE.

THE PEOPLE'S PICTURE PALACE.

TO-DAY & TO-MORROW, at 2-45, 7, and 9—
The Great Masterpieces of Cinematography
"RAISED FROM THE RANKS,"
"FOUNTAIN PEN" "COTTON TIME,"
"A MUDDY ROMANCE,"
"AMID RAGING BEASTS,"
"LITTLE KAINTUCK," 'WHY I AM HERE,'
" GAUMONT," and " Fanny's Conspiracy."

TREMENDOUS, GIGANTIC SUCCESS !

ANOTHER GRAND PROGRAMME

MONDAY NEXT, MARCH 30th, 1914,
and during the week, 2-45, 7, and 9.
At Enormous Cost. Cannot be seen at any
other place.
The Great Race for 1914, **THE**

GRAND NATIONAL.

THE FULL RACE FROM START TO FINISH,
AND **EIGHT OTHER STAR PICTURES,**
Including one of the Best and Most Powerful
Dramas ever produced, viz. :

" A FIGHT FOR A DIAMOND."

**THESE GREAT PICTURES CAN ONLY BE
SEEN AT THE OLYMPIA, Mr. HARRY
YORKE** having secured the **EXCLUSIVE
RIGHTS FOR DARWEN.**

No better Pictures could possibly be Exhibited
than those at the Olympia.

POPULAR PRICES—

Private Box Seats, **1s.** each. Popular Lounge,
6d. Centre Stalls, **4d.** Pit Stalls, **3d.** **No Early
Doors. TWICE NIGHTLY, 7 and 9.**

MATINEE DAILY, at 2-45. N.B.—Afternoon Tea will be served **Free** in the 6d. and 1s.
Seats.

Children under 12, Half-price.

NOTE.—Pit Entrance only, in Foundry-street.

SMOKING ALLOWED, ALL PARTS.

Where Everybody Now Goes to Enjoy a Clean
Entertainment to suit all classes—

THE POPULAR OLYMPIA.

Friday March 27th 1914

New Garden Village Built

SPRING VALE GARDEN VILLAGE was the dream of the Davies family, who decided to provide improved housing for their workers and others who needed homes. They were devout Quakers and probably influenced by what the Cadbury family had done at Bournville.

Many mill owners constructed rows of terraced houses close to their

mills but the Davies family wanted to provide houses with gardens in a pleasant setting, each having a bath and their own toilet. The Davies family were owners of the Greenfield Mill Company, originally begun by E. M. Davies and T. P. Davies sons of the Rev. T. Davies, minister at Duckworth Street Congregational Church. Percy Davies was the son of T. P. Davies and he went to a Quaker School at Sidcot where in 1898 he met Corder Catchpool and they became friends. Percy persuaded his father to appoint Corder Catchpool as resident engineer at their works and also to spend time looking at the social welfare of their workers.

Corder Catchpool made his home at No. 3, having been recently married this was his first home. He stayed there for 10 years and left just a week or two before Gandhi visited.

Eventually a plan was drawn up to build 100 houses to be let to the workers of Greenfield Mills and also to others who needed homes, on 8½ acres, formally part of Greenfield Farm. The foundation stone was laid in 1913 by Mrs Elizabeth Davies who was presented with a silver trowel. By the summer of 1914 the first 30 houses were built, but then the First World War held up further development. A further 30 houses were built later.

Houses with parlours cost £600 each and those without parlours cost £490 and the rents were 9s5d and 7s4d. There was a variety of styles of houses and on the village green there was a sundial.

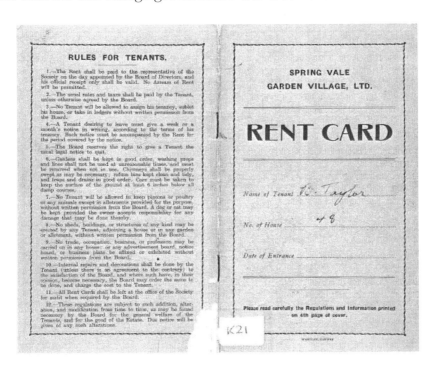

Spring Bank School Opened

SPRING BANK SCHOOL opened on August 17th 1914 and was the second school in Darwen provided by Lancashire County Council. It was opened a fortnight after the beginning of the First World War and there was the possibility of it becoming a hospital for wounded soldiers, but this did no happen. It was, like Sudell Road School, an Elementary School taking pupils from 7 years to 13 years, with the  half-time system still in operation in the final year. In 1933 it became a Secondary Modern School and today it is a primary school.

Jubilee of St John's Church

ST JOHN'S CHURCH was consecrated on July 7th 1864 by the Bishop of Manchester. The Reverend Philip Graham and Mrs Graham (widow of Eccles Shorrock and formally Miss Brandwood of Turncroft) had generously given funds for the construction of the church, amounting to £8,000, and also given the land on which it was built.

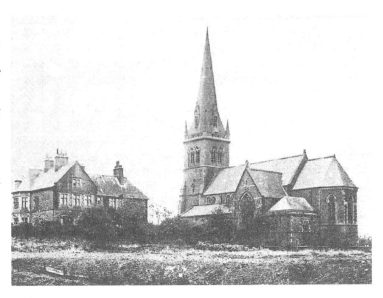

The Rev. Philip Graham became the first vicar of St John's and was now living at Turncroft Hall, his wife's previous family home. He had earlier been a curate at Holy Trinity Church, then later in Manchester. The parish of St John's was created out of the parish of Holy Trinity, and included the mission districts of Grimehills and St Barnabas.

The Church was given various additions and alterations for the Jubilee:

The restoration of the organ

The removal of old ventilation and the installation of a fan

The laying of the Chancel floor with marble

Cleaning and decoration of the interior

Laying out of the churchyard

Repairs to the exterior

Mr Thomas Knowles, J.P., provided electric lighting and fittings

Mr and Mrs J. T. Hargreaves presented a new oak Altar

Some of the ladies raised funds for new Altar linen, silk bookmarkers and a new Bible for the Lectern

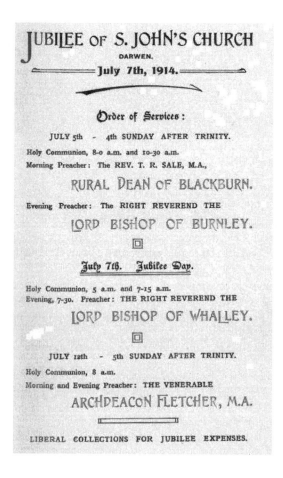

Moss Bridge Hospital

MOSS BRIDGE HOUSE was the home of Gordon Shorrock. He donated the house to be converted into a military hospital for wounded soldiers at the beginning of World War I. Local tradesmen provided their services free of charge and began alterations on August 15th 1914.

The first contingent of wounded Belgian soldiers arrived at the hospital on October 20th. The Mayor, Alderman James Cocker, met the soldiers at Darwen station and a fleet of motor cars took them to the hospital. The route was lined with thousands of people, greeting the soldiers and showering them with cigarettes and flowers. The hospital contained 20 beds and nurses from St John Ambulance Brigade were trained to care for them.

OTHER EVENTS

Fire at Woodside Mill on March 29th. Damage £15,000

War August 4th

Over 30 mills closed August 13th

A new type of carboniser was erected at the Gas Works and was the first of its kind in the country. It became known as the "Darwen Inclined Chamber" oven

Associations and Clubs

Agricultural Association

Allotments Association

Amateur Photographic Society

Angling Association

Brass Bands—Darwen Borough Band, Pickup Bank Band, Salvation Army Band

Church Lads' Brigade

District Nursing Association

Floral and Horticultural Society

Friendly Societies—Oddfellows, Orange Institute, Free Gardeners

Lifeboat Association

Literary Society

Masons

Model Yacht Club

Naturalists Society

N.S.P.C.C

Orchestral Society

Political Associations—Conservative Club, Liberal Club

Scottish Association

Scouts

Spinners Association

Sports Clubs—Athletics (Schoolboy), Billiards, Bowling, Cricket, Cycling, Football, Golf, Gymnastics, Swimming, Tennis

Spring Vale Rambling Class

St Georges Society

Temperance Society

United Irish Club

Weavers Association

Y.M.C.A

This list shows the diversity and variety of activities available to the people of Darwen in this period of time.

PUBLIC HALLS

Co-operative Hall—School Street

Industrial Hall—School Street

Public Hall—Church Street

Provident Hall—The Green

Whalley Chambers—Bridge Street

Eccles' Rooms—Market Street

Bolton Road Assembly Room—Conservative Club

Temperance Working Men's Clubs—Duckworth Street and Redearth Road

Theatre Royal—Church Street

Y.M.C.A—Church Street

Lecture Hall—Technical School

Union Street Assembly Room

Wardley's Rooms—Green Street

Date Stones

THESE ARE PHOTOGRAPHS of some date plaques on garden fronted terraced houses along Blackburn Road. These, built in 1902 the time of the Coronation of Edward VII, were named to reflect the feeling for royalty at that time. There are more date plaques along Blackburn Road and on many other roads in the town.

The Co-operative Society built many terraced houses and in Moorland Avenue the date stone can be seen with the Co-op initials underneath the date. The houses were built at the same time as the Sunnyhurst branch at the top of the road.

All on Earnsdale Road

PROMINENT PEOPLE

In this section there is information on the lives of some prominent people of this period.

HENRY DEAKIN ASHTON 1861-1925

DR J. T. BALLANTYNE 1845-1917

ALEXANDER CARUS 1842-1920

JOHN CATLOW 1840-1910

JOHN CHADWICK b.1830

JAMES COCKER 1850-1935

ERNEST MORGAN DAVIES 1848-1929

THOMAS PIERCE DAVIES 1852-1934

ALEXANDER THOMAS ECCLES 1851-1934

WILLIAM PICKUP HALLIWELL 1864-1925

FREDERICK GEORGE HINDLE 1848-1925

FREDERICK HINDLE 1877-1953

GEORGE PICKUP HOLDEN 1863-1934

CHARLES PHILIP HUNTINGTON 1833-1906

WILLIAM BALLE HUNTINGTON 1841-1911

WALMSLEY PRESTON KAY 1863-1916

JOHN KNOWLES 1814-1908

THOMAS KNOWLES 1844-1924

NATHANIEL LEACH 1849-1945

TIMOTHY LIGHTBOWN 1838-1910

JOHN PICKUP 1864-1926

COLONEL WILLIAM HENRY PLACE 1848-1919

JOHN JOSEPH RILEY 1851-1925

COLONEL JOHN RUTHERFORD 1854-1932

RALPH SHORROCK 1836-1916

ROBERT SHORROCK 1855-1932

ROBERT WILLIAM SMITH-SAVILLE 1867-1915

JAMES TOMLINSON 1838-1917

JOHN TOMLINSON 1846-1922

JOHN WARDLEY 1835-1912

GEORGE YATES 1860-1929

RALPH YATES 1857-1934

HENRY DEAKIN ASHTON 1861-1925

HENRY DEAKIN ASHTON was the son of William Thomas Ashton and he and his brothers carried on their father's work to secure the freedom of the moors for the townspeople of Darwen. He lived at Ellerslie and wanted to make the extensive grounds of his home into a sanctuary for birds and animals. He was originally a Liberal but became a Conservative and was a Congregationalist worshipping at Belgrave Church. He died of pneumonia aged 64 years. His business was in cotton manufacturing at Hope and Whitehall weaving mills.

Ellerslie 2010

DR J. T. BALLANTYNE 1845-1917

DR JAMES TODD BALLANTYNE came to Darwen in 1880 from Glasgow. He lived at Holker House and had a surgery in Green Street. He was a Liberal and entered the Town Council on November 1st 1894. He was one of the earliest members of the Literary

Society and was also a Freemason, a member of the Golf Club and of a Caledonian Curling Club in Blackburn. He started a fund to raise money for the wives and families of reservists called upon to serve in the Boer War. In his Mayoral year, a portrait in oils was painted of him by his cousin John Shields, who unfortunately died before he could finish it, so his executors had it completed. Dr Ballantyne set to work to design a frame for the portrait, and then spent many years carving it himself. He did not quite finish it but his executors decided to leave it as it was.

Holker House

211

ALEXANDER CARUS 1842-1920

ALEXANDER CARUS WAS A native of Blackburn but lived in Hoddlesden for many years, mostly at Hoddlesden Hall. He went to a private school and began work as a clerk to solicitors. After four years he gave up law and entered the cotton business. In 1882 he bought St Paul's Mill, Hoddlesden, and became one of the largest cotton manufacturers in the district. He was a

Liberal and served on the Town Council for 30 years becoming Darwen's first Catholic Mayor and was made a Freeman of the Borough in 1920. He was prominently associated with St Joseph's Church and the Catholic Club and was made a Knight of St Gregory, an honour bestowed by the Pope. In 1895-96 he was President of the Literary Society. He enjoyed travelling and visited America and India. He was prominent in promoting the construction of a tram line to Hoddlesden.

Hoddlesden Hall

JOHN CATLOW 1840-1910

JOHN CATLOW CAME FROM Chapels and his parents died when he was very young leaving him an orphan. He began his working life at Dob Meadows Printworks and was later employed at various local mills,

working hard in all aspects of the cotton trade. In 1874, he became a tackler and junior partner at Springfield Mill, Bolton Road. He took over Radford Mill in 1889, Olive Lane Mill in 1894 and Anchor Mill in 1900. By 1914, the firm he had established, John Catlow and Sons, was working five weaving mills. His workforce had increased from 150 to 500-600 in the space of 11 years. He died at his home, The Serpentine, in Lytham but had previously lived at Dunkeld House in Whitehall Road.

Dunkeld House, Whitehall Road

Mr J. H. Catlow

His son James Henry Catlow lived at The Firs, Whitehall Road.

The Firs, Whitehall Road (now Moorlands)

213

JOHN CHADWICK b. 1830

JOHN CHADWICK WAS BORN in 1830 at a shop in Market Street. His family were butchers and at that time there were only two other butchers in the town. His shop was Nos. 9 and 11 Albert Buildings. When he went to Skipton market, he used to travel on horseback with a group of other butchers from Bolton and Darwen. They travelled overnight and in those days it was a dangerous journey so they felt there was safety in numbers. He became quite prosperous and lived at Highfield House. As well as the gateway he donated to Sunnyhurst Wood, he also donated a flag pole to Bold Venture Park which was made of iron as wood tended to decay. It was 15 feet high and cost £15.

Highfield House, Brandwood Street

JAMES COCKER 1850-1935

JAMES COCKER WAS BORN AT Stoney Flatts in a hairdresser's shop next door to the Sun Hotel. His father Samuel Cocker, formerly a handloom weaver, started business as a coal dealer and at the age of seven years, James helped to take the coal to his father's customers. When

he was older he got a job with John Knowles, building contractor, whom he succeeded in the business. He was educated at Eccles Shorrock old Factory School in Astley Street, then at Belgrave School and finally at the Mechanics Institute. He was a Liberal and Member of the Town Council for 46 years, holding the positions of magistrates, alderman, Mayor (five times), and was made Honorary Freeman in 1920. He was a great benefactor to the Primitive Methodist Church, working in both the church and the Sunday school. He married Miss Knowles, daughter of John Knowles and lived at Inglewood, Whitehall Road.

Inglewood, Whitehall Road

215

ERNEST MORGAN DAVIES 1848-1929

ERNEST MORGAN DAVIES WAS the eldest son of the Rev Thomas Davies, minister at Duckworth Street Congregational Church. The family originally came from Wales, but Ernest was born at Maidenhead. He was a pupil at Blackburn Grammar School and later learnt the cotton trade at Peel Mill, Preston. His father bought Greenfield Mill and he and his younger brother ran that mill and Waterfield Mill. He was a staunch Congregationalist and member of Duckworth Street Church, where he had filled every office, and also was a founder member of Hollins Grove and Highfield Churches. In 1884, he entered the Town Council and was a member for over 20 years, being appointed Mayor in 1889-1891. He enjoyed cycling, walking, motoring, foreign travel and music. He lived at Moorthorpe, Whitehall.

Moorthorpe, Whitehall

THOMAS PIERCE DAVIES 1852-1934

THOMAS PIERCE DAVIES was the younger brother of Ernest Morgan Davies. Like his brother, he worked hard for Duckworth Street Congregational Church and had an absorbing interest in foreign mission work. He was a member of the Town Council and in 1905 became Mayor. He was one of the early members of Darwen Literary Society. Just before the first World War he was instrumental in building a garden village at Spring Vale. He was a good business man and interested in the lives and conditions of those who worked for him at Greenfield Mill. In Darwen he lived at Heatherfield, in Whitehall Road, then in 1919 went to live at Grange over Sands. His two sons J. Percival and William R. took over the running of Greenfield Mill. J. Percival, known as Percy, was very interested in the welfare of the workforce and in 1946 was created a Baron, known as Baron Darwen of Heys in Bowland.

Now Astley House, but research points to this previously being Heatherfield

217

ALEXANDER THOMAS ECCLES 1851-1934

ALEXANDER THOMAS ECCLES was born in Union Street. He was the son of Joseph Eccles who was a cotton manufacturer with his brother Thomas, at Bottomcroft Mill. Their partnership was dissolved in 1903 and A. T. Eccles and Sons was formed to run the Darwen Mills. Alexander's elder brother Joseph, took over the Preston mills. For many years Alexander was a member of the Town Council, becoming an Alderman in 1890 and was Mayor three times. He retired from the Council in 1920, at which time he was their oldest member and on retirement was made a Freeman of the Borough. He was responsible for the building of Hollins Grove Chapel and lived at "The Grange" which was next to the Chapel

on the Oldfield Avenue side. The congregation of the Chapel presented him with his portrait in oils in recognition for his 48 years service. He entertained Lord Morley at his house when he came to address a Liberal meeting in 1910. There was a demonstration by suffragettes and some hid in the bushes in the grounds of his house. He died at his home in Grange-over-Sands having previously lived on the Isle of Anglesey where he had been made High Sheriff.

The Grange, Oldfield Avenue

WILLIAM PICKUP HALLIWELL 1864-1925

WILLIAM PICKUP HALLIWELL was the second son of James Halliwell, cotton manufacturer at George Street Mill. When he was 10 years old he went to Blackburn Grammar School and in 1887 gained his B.A. at London University. He became a solicitor practising in Railway Road and entered into partnership with his brother, R. S. Halliwell. In 1900, he became the Town Clerk for Darwen, a position he occupied for 23 years. He was a strong supporter of Duckworth Street Congregational Church and was a teacher in the Sunday school. When Highfield Church was built he attended there and held many positions of responsibility. He was a member of the Literary Society, he enjoyed sport and was fond of travel. He never married and lived at Craigside then at Newhaven at the top of Ashleigh Street.

Craigside, Ashleigh Street

219

FREDERICK GEORGE HINDLE 1848-1925

FREDERICK GEORGE HINDLE was probably born at Hoddlesden and his family were of yeoman stock. He was educated at the old Blackburn Grammar School in Freckleton Street and had to walk a distance of four miles each way to school. Darwen boys later became boarders. In 1865 he was articled to Mr Charles Kendall who was clerk to the magistrates and to the local Board of Health. He passed his final examinations as a solicitor in 1870, coming at the head of the honours list for the whole of England. For two years he was apprenticed in Manchester and Bolton, then he commenced practice in his native town establishing himself as one of the ablest lawyers of his day. In 1881 he was appointed Clerk to the Justices, a position he held until his death. He fought for Free Trade and against Protection and was elected a Member of Parliament on this issue.

He was a staunch Liberal and in 1885 was the agent for J. G. Potter when he lost the election to Lord Cranborne. The first victory for Darwen Liberals was in 1892 and won by Mr C. P. Huntington who was greatly helped by Mr Hindle. He, himself, became Member of Parliament in 1910 but held the seat for less than a year.

In 1897, acting for the sons of W. T. Ashton, he successfully dealt with the legalities of gaining public access to the moors. He was a good all-round sportsman, enjoying cycling, swimming, tennis and golf. For 20 years he held a commission in the Volunteer Force, holding the honorary rank of Major.

He was an authority on licensing laws and an advocate of temperance, leading the way in closing many beer shops. He married

Helen, the daughter of Thomas Gillibrand of Hollins Grove House. They lived at Thorncliffe but then in 1910 moved to Astley Bank.

Astley Bank

He was a member of Belgrave Church and was fond of saying "he was not a pillar of the church but one of the flying buttresses." In 1917 he was awarded a testimonial from the Royal Humane Society for the rescue of a young lady who was drowning in the sea at Llandudno. He died at Nice in the South of France.

From left to right: Standing Mr Joseph Hindle, Mr F. G. Hindle, Mr John Hindle and Mr Thomas Hindle Second row: Mr William Hindle and Miss Jane Hindle Third row: Mrs Hindle and Mr John Hindle, with Mr E. J. Hindle kneeling in front

FREDERICK HINDLE 1877-1953

FREDERICK, SOMETIMES known as Fritz, had a distinguished career in the legal profession like his father Frederick George Hindle. He passed the advanced law examinations with distinction and was awarded the Vice-Chancellor's prize for the most successful law student of his year. In the final examination for solicitors, he was the only student of his year to gain first class honours. In 1899 he entered into partnership with his father and Mr James Cooper.

He was a member of Darwen Council as Councillor and Alderman for 25 years, leaving when he became Magistrates' Clerk, succeeding his father. In 1907 he was elected a member of Lancashire County Council. As a Liberal, he became Member of Parliament for Darwen in 1923 and later in 1943 he was knighted for "public services to Lancashire".

He continued to live at Astley Bank, his family home, after he was married.

In 1914, although above enlistment age, he went to France with his car and his father's car both of which had been fitted up as ambulances. He remained with the British in Flanders for about 18 months and was then transferred to the French army where he was given a commission. He was in the thick of severe fighting and after being

Father and son outside Astley Bank

mentioned in despatches, he was invested on the battlefield with the Croix de Guerre for the gallant part he played in the defence of Verdun. In 1917 he was awarded a bar to the Croix de Guerre for rescuing, under heavy fire, a French flying officer. Shortly afterwards he was given a commission with the British army. For his four years service in France he received the Mons medal, ribbon and chevron.

GEORGE PICKUP HOLDEN 1863-1934

GEORGE PICKUP HOLDEN was educated at Blackburn Grammar School and left school in 1878 when he went into Bank Top Mill with his father. He took over the business on his own in 1891 and at one period was also in business at Atlas Mill. He entered the

Town Council in 1902 and retired in 1926. In politics he was a Conservative, but had previously been a Liberal. He was made a Justice of the Peace in 1905 and Mayor in 1907-08. He attended Holy Trinity Church and was an organist of no mean ability. He was an early member and a President of the Literary Society. He was instrumental in seeing the Higher Grade School established and was given a seat on the School Board. He travelled to Finland and Russia and knew Germany well. His daughter married a Kapitan Leutenant in the German Admiralty.

He lived at Spring Bank which had been rebuilt in 1898. He married Annie, daughter of John Brown of Dumfries and when she died he married the widow of G. G. Sames, the architect. He died at his home in Ambleside.

Spring Bank (Whitehall Hotel)

CHARLES PHILIP HUNTINGTON 1833-1906

CHARLES PHILIP HUNTINGTON was born at Mitcham in Surrey and he came to Darwen in 1864. He had been well educated and had a high reputation for drawing and as a colourist. He and his brothers, James and William Balle came to Darwen at the invitation of Potters of Belgrave Mills. Charles came to be a wallpaper designer and took charge of the art department. His interest in politics was as a Liberal and he contested the general election in 1892 and defeated Lord Cranborne. Later in 1895, he was defeated by Mr J. Rutherford. He opened the Higher Grade School in 1894 and gave £1000 to be invested and to provide an annual prize. In 1906 he was created a baronet but died later that year. He lived at Astley Bank in Darwen, but later moved to The Clock House on the Chelsea embankment where he died.

Astley Bank

WILLIAM BALLE HUNTINGTON 1841-1911

LIKE HIS BROTHERS, Charles and James, William came to Darwen from Mitchum in Surrey at the invitation of Potters of Belgrave. At first he lived at Orchard Bank (Alexandra Hotel) then he moved to Woodlands. In 1884 he founded the Huntington Lectures which became one of the educational features of the town. The Industrial Co-operative Society had a series of Gilchrist Trust Lectures delivered in the Co-op Hall. These were very popular but at the end of the second season were unable to continue. William Balle Huntington offered to pay the cost of lectures for three years, at the end of which he offered to pay for another three years. In 1897, in honour of Queen Victoria's Jubilee, he made a permanent endowment of £2,000 in trust for the lectures. There were many interesting and varied topics and many famous speakers such as Jerome K. Jerome, John Masefield, G. K. Chesterton, Hilaire Belloc and many more.

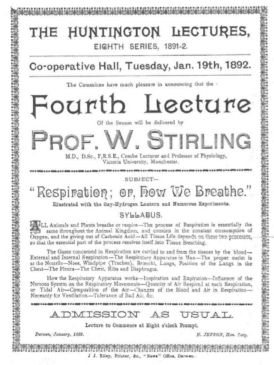

The Cover of the "William Huntington Lectures."
Endowed by W. B. Huntington, Esquire, D.L., J.P., at a cost of £2,000, in Commemoration of the Diamond Jubilee. Cover designed by Walter Crane.

Woodlands

William B. Huntington was a Conservative and became a Justice of the Peace but never became involved in local politics. In 1898 he was made High Sheriff for the County Palatine of Lancashire. This was the first time someone from Darwen was given this high honour. There was an official procession from Woodlands to Blackburn Railway Station where he caught the train to Manchester.

The High Sheriff's procesion at the bottom of Bolton Road

He later lived in Piccadilly, London and at Blackmore Park, Worcester where he died.

His elder son was Arthur William Huntington who entered the firm of "Potters" as a partner in 1892 and after the formation of The Wall Paper Manufacturers Ltd., became a director of the company. (On his initiative experiments were made for the production of a water paint which later lead to the formation of Walpamur). He went to South Africa to fight in the Boer War where he won the D.S.O. and was made a Major.

Major A. W. Huntington
D.L., J.P., D.S.O.

WALMSLEY PRESTON KAY 1863-1916

WALMSLEY PRESTON KAY was related to Walmsley Preston through his father, Andrew Kay. (Andrew Kay, who married Elizabeth Walmsley, daughter of Alderman Walmsley, was the son of John Kay whose sister, Ann, was married to Walmsley Preston).

Walmsley Preston Kay married Jeanie Ross-Brown from Scotland and they lived at Higher Croft at Lower Darwen. He began his education under the tuition of Mr James Hargreaves and then went to a private school in Mellor and then one in Hoghton. He was educated with a view to a career in the law and aged 16 he was articled to a firm in Bolton and then to one in London. In 1882 he became a solicitor and at first went into partnership with a relative and then practised on his own. He became a Councillor in 1903 and was Chairman of the Finance Committee. He was Mayor for two years 1909-1911. He was a lifelong teetotaller and was President of Darwen and District Band of Hope and Temperance Union. He was prominently associated with the United Methodist Free Church at Duckworth Street and at Lower Darwen. His other interests were the Literary Society, the Nursing Association and the Psychical Society, as he was interested in metaphysics. He died in Scotland when staying with relatives for Christmas. Dr Ballantyne had rushed to Scotland to attend to him.

Higher Croft, Lower Darwen

JOHN KNOWLES 1814-1908

JOHN KNOWLES CAME TO Darwen as a child and later started work with Richard Thompson, a builder, working on Radford Hall. He became a skilled stonemason and started his own business at Thorney Height quarry. He became the largest contractor in Darwen and was responsible for many of the town's most important buildings. Some of these were: Bank Terrace, India Mill, Darwen Spinning Mill, New Mill, Vale Mount, and alterations to Spring Bank, Woodlands, Astley Bank, Ashdale, Thorncliffe, Parkside, Dunkeld, Radford Bank, Oldfield, Ellerslie, extensions to Low Hill, and many railway bridges. For most of his life John Knowles lived at Radfield Head. When he was 93 years old he was walking across the Circus and was knocked down by a horse and trap. He died a few days later from the injuries he sustained, including a broken hip.

Radfield Head

Established 1873.

JOHN KNOWLES,

Contractor .
Plumber, and
Builders' . . .
Merchant. . .

CENTRAL AND BOLTON ROAD

TIMBER YARDS AND SAW MILLS.

... DARWEN.

Telephone No. 53.

THOMAS KNOWLES 1844-1924

THOMAS KNOWLES STARTED work on the railways at 13 years of age as a number taker. He worked 14 hours a day for three shillings a week. In 1870 to 1876 he became the station master at Sough. He left the railway in 1876 and took up the position of secretary to Messrs Ralph Entwistle and Co. Ltd., sanitary pipe manufacturers of Cranberry lane, and in 12 months time he became manager as well as secretary. In 1888 he left and bought Spring Vale Fire Brick Works where he began making sanitary goods and remained there until his death. He was a consistent worker for the Conservative party and a committed member of St John's Church. He died at his home, Lyndene in Ashleigh Street.

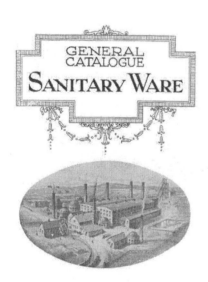

GENERAL CATALOGUE
SANITARY WARE

THOMAS KNOWLES
LIMITED
SPRING VALE STONEWARE WORKS
DARWEN, Lancs.

Phone—55 DARWEN   Grams—"KNOWLES, 55 DARWEN"

Lyndene, Ashleigh Street

Frontispiece from a Thomas Knowles Catalogue. The illustration shows the pipe works and its associated collieries.
(By permission of Lancashire Libraries)

NATHANIEL LEACH 1849-1945

NATHANIEL LEACH WAS THE proprietor of the Darwen Weekly Advertiser. He began in business on his own in 1880 at premises in Bolton Road where Springfield Mill formerly stood. In 1892, owing to increased business, new premises were built across the road known as Caxton Works, where a year later he published the Darwen Weekly Advertiser. He attended Lower Chapel Church but took no part in municipal matters. His son, Eli Leach, who predeceased him in 1938, was Mayor of the Borough in 1928-1929. Nathaniel died aged 96 years and was the oldest Master Printer in the country. He lived at Pendle View (now Denehurst) on Tockholes Road and his son lived further down the road at "The Crest".

The Crest, Tockholes Road

Pendle View (now Denehurst), Tockholes Road

231

TIMOTHY LIGHTBOWN 1838-1910

TIMOTHY LIGHTBOWN WAS BORN in an old farmhouse on Darwen moor called Clam Belly Hall. (The original occupant was a relieving officer who was known to deal harshly with those who applied to him for relief—hence the name). When Timothy was three years old, his father, a handloom weaver, decided to emigrate with his family to America. The family were in America for 21 years and did very well. Timothy became a teacher and then took his Bachelor of Arts degree. At the onset of the American Civil War the family decided to return to Darwen in 1861. Timothy and his brother Roger set up in business as cotton manufacturers at Dove Mill. Timothy married the adopted daughter of Walmsley Preston and lived at Falcon House. It was a happy marriage, but they had no children. He was a Liberal in politics and in religion a non-conformist, worshipping at Belgrave Independent Meeting House. His career in public life was very distinguished and in 1906 he received the honorary Freedom of the Borough, the first person to do so. On his death he left £10,000 to benefit the people of Darwen.

Falcon House, Falcon Avenue (now the Liberal Club)

JOHN PICKUP 1864-1926

JOHN PICKUP AND HIS family were closely associated with the farming industry, he was a gentleman farmer. He was the son of Alderman William Pickup who was Mayor in 1894-1895. John Pickup

entered public life in 1899 as a Councillor and in 1911-1912 became Mayor. His expertise was on Highways, Waterworks and Land Purchases. He was a Liberal and attended Duckworth Street Congregational Church. He took over Progress Mill and also spent time re-working the coal pits on his estate. He lived at Lower Marsh House which is now a private day nursery.

Lower Marsh House, Marsh House Lane

COLONEL WILLIAM HENRY PLACE
1848-1919

WILLIAM HENRY PLACE was head of the family business Joseph Place and Sons Ltd., making pipes and brick. He was the son of Joseph Place and ran the business with his brother John Edwin. For 26 years 1875-1901 he was a popular officer in the Volunteer Force and was an expert rifle shot. He excelled in cricket, football and later golf and was an accomplished tenor vocalist. He lived at Ashleigh.

Ashleigh, Ashleigh Street

JOHN JOSEPH RILEY 1851-1925

JOHN JOSEPH RILEY came to Darwen in 1860 from the Leeds area with his widowed mother and sisters. He began work as an errand boy and later became an apprentice with Mr Gregson whose businesses were as a druggist, a printer and a postmaster. He was educated at Darwen Mechanics Institute, attending night classes. In 1871 when Mr Gregson died he took over the business as a printer in his own right and his first premises were at No. 1 Union Street. In 1875 he found it necessary to purchase the block on the corner of Market Street and Union Street. From 1871 to 1881 he concentrated on developing a general commercial printing business, then he purchased the Darwen News which had been established in 1874. The growth of the newspaper and the development of the

Whitehall Bank, Whitehall Road

printing business justified acquiring new works. In 1885 he purchased land known as William Street Yard and a new model printing works was erected. In 1897, the editorial department of the paper transferred to new and spacious offices in Duckworth Street.

He was a pioneer of Methodism

and worshipped at Bolton Road Methodist Church. In politics he was a Liberal. He lived at Whitehall Bank in Whitehall Road. J. J. Riley came from a poor background but became one of the leading newspaper proprietors in North East Lancashire, also establishing businesses in Rossendale and Southport.

COLONEL JOHN RUTHERFORD 1854-1932

JOHN RUTHERFORD WAS of Scottish descent but was born in Blackburn. His father established Salford Brewery with Mr Henry Shaw. He went to Lancaster Grammar School and then to Glasgow University.

On his father's death he took over the management of the business and also became Vice-Chairman of Daniel Thwaites and Co. Ltd. He was an Alderman and an ex-Mayor of the Borough of Blackburn. In 1895 he became Conservative Member of Parliament for Darwen, a position he held for 25 years, apart from a brief period in 1910. He was a member of the Jockey Club and a successful owner of steeplechasers. For 30

years he served in the Duke of Lancaster's Own Yeomanry and was given command of the troops in 1901. He had a national reputation as a grower of rare orchids. He lived at Beardwood in Blackburn, now a hospital, and remained a bachelor all his life. A peerage was bestowed upon him in 1915.

Beardwood, Preston New Road, Blackburn

RALPH SHORROCK 1836-1916

RALPH SHORROCK WAS BORN at Spring Vale and then moved to Union Street. When he was eight years old he worked at New Mill. He was then sent to William Street School where education was provided by Eccles Shorrock and Co., for the benefit of workpeople and their families. When he was 17 years old he left the mill and apprenticed himself to a cousin, Richard Shorrock to learn the business of chemist and druggist. Just as he finished his apprenticeship, Richard died leaving a widow and two children. Ralph took charge of the business and after 18 months he married the widow. When he was well-established he decided to become a dentist. He became one of the earliest to practice dentistry. He trained with a friend, Mr Deane, in Manchester and stayed with him for three years. He attended Belgrave Congregational Church where he became a Senior Deacon and was a manager of the Day School for over 30 years. He was a member of the Town Council and was made an Alderman and Mayor in 1906-1907. He had many interests, being a keen horticulturalist, setting up the Athletics Club, being an enthusiastic cricketer and a member of the Choral Society. He was a Freemason and a member of the Literary Society. He lived at Newhaven at the top of Ashleigh Street and was married three times. Newhaven is no longer standing and new apartments have been built in its place.

Dentistry With all The Recent Improvements

Teeth Carefully Extracted.

ARTIFICIAL TEETH

PERFECT FIT GUARANTEED.

All Branches of Mechanical Dentistry conducted on the Premises

Established over 30 years.

CHARGES VERY MODERATE, and Consultations Free.
in accordance with Materials used.

RALPH SHORROCK,
(REGISTERED),
SURGEON DENTIST,
6, Market St., Darwen.

Site of Newhaven, Ashleigh Street

ROBERT SHORROCK 1855-1932

ROBERT SHORROCK WAS BORN at Mill Farm behind Darwen Paper Mill. He was the youngest of 15 children and the son of Ralph Shorrock, engineer and farmer. As a youth he went to work in the engineering shop of Lea Foundry (Messrs J. & R. Shorrock) but later took to carpentry and became a joiner in Union Street. In 1877, he founded the firm of Shorrock and Sons Ltd., contractors and timber merchants of Union Street Saw Mills. His firm carried out the enlargement of the works of Messrs Howard and Bullough, Accrington, which amounted to a quarter of a million pounds. In Darwen his firm were contractors for: the Post Office, the Public Library, Manchester and County Bank, Marsh House Mill, Cobden Mill, Peel Mill, Premier Mill, St Georges Church, Hollins Grove Congregational Church, Highfield Church, Avondale Girls School and many other buildings. In 1897, he gained a seat on the Town Council and in 1902 he became Mayor. He was a Liberal and attended Belgrave Congregational Church. He lived at Heatherby (near Astley Bank) and at Moorhurst, Ashleigh Street.

Moorhurst, Ashleigh Street

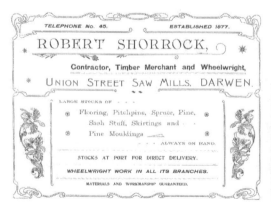

Heatherby (near Astley Bank)

238

ROBERT WILLIAM SMITH-SAVILLE
1867-1915

ROBERT WILLIAM SMITH-SAVILLE came to Darwen in 1896 when he was appointed Borough Surveyor and Engineer. He carried out some very important schemes and held the positions of Waterworks Engineer, Engineering Manager of the Tramways Department and Architect to the Education Committee. He held responsibility for the construction of the sewage works, the tramway to Hoddlesden, the refuse destructor, the waterworks extensions, the parks, the erection of two council schools, Bull Hill Hospital extensions, Belgrave Square, three bowling greens and many more smaller projects. He enjoyed organising public functions and was active in all spheres except politics. He became President of the Literary Society and worshipped at St Cuthbert's Church.

It was said that he had a racy style and his original ideas and fearless comments were always listened to with pleasure and interest by his colleagues. He had an accident on a tramcar and later, when in London, he was taken ill suddenly. Though he returned to work for a few weeks, he was taken ill again and died aged 48 years at his home, 8 Hawkshaw Avenue, leaving a widow, two sons and a daughter.

8 Hawkshaw Avenue

JAMES TOMLINSON 1838-1917

JAMES TOMLINSON WAS BORN at Chapels. When he was eight years old he went to Dob Meadows Dyeing and Bleaching Works where he worked from 5 am till 10 or 11 o'clock at night for three shillings a week. When possible he was allowed to attend Willow Street School. Nine years later he worked in a cotton mill and then he was employed at William Street Ropery. Later he became the caretaker at Belgrave Independent Chapel for nine years. He then acquired the Willow Street Works and went into business on his own

account, also acquiring Spring Vale Ropery and trading under the title of Messrs James Tomlinson and Sons. In 1895 he gained a seat on the Town Council where he gave unbroken service for 22 years. In 1904 he was elected to be Chief Magistrate of the Borough and was Mayor in 1904-1905. In politics he was a Liberal and he attended Belgrave Congregational Church. He was a musician of considerable ability, playing in the Temperance Band, and was an Oddfellow, a Mason and a member of two bowling clubs. He lived at Belgrave Cottage and then at No. 7 Church Terrace.

No. 7 Church Terrace

Belgrave Cottage, Belgrave Road

JOHN TOMLINSON 1846-1922

FROM SMALL BEGINNINGS John Tomlinson established a coal business which developed into control of one colliery, a direct interest in others and with distribution depots throughout North East Lancashire. He was a member of the Town Council for 35 years, Mayor of the Borough in 1900-1902 and was made a Borough Justice of the Peace for 30 years and a County Justice of the Peace for 14 years. For a quarter of a century he was a member of the executive of Darwen Liberal Association and in religion was a loyal

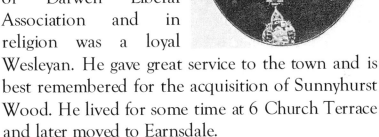

Wesleyan. He gave great service to the town and is best remembered for the acquisition of Sunnyhurst Wood. He lived for some time at 6 Church Terrace and later moved to Earnsdale.

6 Church Terrace 1901

6 Church Terrace 2010

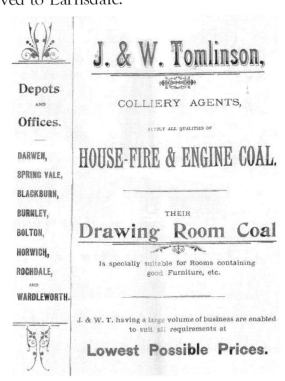

Earnsdale

J. & W. Tomlinson,

Depots AND Offices.

COLLIERY AGENTS,

SUPPLY ALL QUALITIES OF

HOUSE-FIRE & ENGINE COAL.

DARWEN,
SPRING VALE,
BLACKBURN,
BURNLEY,
BOLTON,
HORWICH,
ROCHDALE,
AND
WARDLEWORTH.

THEIR

Drawing Room Coal

Is specially suitable for Rooms containing good Furniture, etc.

J. & W. T. having a large volume of business are enabled to suit all requirements at

Lowest Possible Prices.

J. & W. Tomlinson, largest dealers in coal, cannel, furnace and gas coke in Lancashire. Founded c. 1860s. Home: 6 Church Terrace

JOHN WARDLEY 1835-1912

JOHN WARDLEY WAS BORN at Birkacre Print Works near Chorley where his father was manager of the block printing works. Later the family moved to Crawshawbooth where unfortunately when he was only 6 years old, John's father died. Mrs Wardley and her five children were destitute and as a consequence the family were scattered going to live with various relatives. John went to live with his uncle James in Salford where he received a fair education. When his uncle died, John came to Darwen and joined Messrs Wardley and Sons, calico printers at Spring Vale. The firm prospered until coal mines on Cranberry Moss were re-opened resulting in the pollution of the water (River Darwen), which made it unfit for dyeing purposes. In 1860 John Wardley left the print works and bought the book selling and stationary business of Mr W. A. Briggs at 4 Market Street. Then in 1870 he purchased the business of Mr Edward Gregson, printer and stationer, at 42 Market Street and Arch Street. He was closely associated with printing either on calico or paper all his life and remembered the experiments by the Potters of trying to print wallpaper on the adapted calico printing machines at Spring Vale. In 1884 he entered the Town Council representing the Liberal Party. In 1897 he was made an Alderman and in 1902 a Justice of the Peace. He worshipped at Belgrave Meeting House and was a member of the choir there. He was a member of the Literary Society and a very committed member of the Freemasons, receiving various honours.

43 Sudell Road

He was succeeded in business by his son, Charles.

GEORGE YATES 1860-1929

GEORGE YATES WAS BORN in Belthorn and was of humble parentage. He went to work in the mill and received a sparse education. He then took up a position as clerk at Cotton Hall and later became secretary of the Albert Spinning Mill Co. Ltd. He left the mill

to set up business on his own account as a yarn agent. He acquired premises above the Manchester and County Bank in 1900. His success was rapid and he established a business of extended proportions and became a familiar figure at the Cotton Exchange, Manchester, being well-known generally in the cotton trade in the county. His public life was devoted to religion, politics and literature. He held many offices at Duckworth Street Congregational Church and throughout his life worked hard for the Sunday School and Church. He had a love of literature and was a capable debater, speaker and able writer. In 1900 he was President of the Literary Society where he

spoke on many varied subjects, one of which was "George Eliot as a Novelist". He organised the art exhibition in the Library in 1912. In

Woodlands

politics he was a staunch Liberal and he promoted Liberal propaganda throughout the constituency but did not stand for the Town Council. For many years he was Borough Auditor and was appointed a Borough Magistrate and a County Magistrate. He was a member of the Free Trade League and published a pamphlet to promote Free Trade against Tariff Reform. One of his chief delights was the study of horticulture and he was usually seen wearing a buttonhole. He married Nancy Yates, sister of Ralph Yates, Cotton Waste dealer and they lived at Woodlands which he bought from his friend E. M. Davies.

RALPH YATES 1857-1934

RALPH YATES WAS BORN in Lower Darwen and was educated at Belgrave and Duckworth Street Day Schools. He became a clerk at Belgrave Mills when he was 15 years old and studied languages at evening school. At the age of 18 years, he began to develop the family cotton waste business with his brother Edward and later joined by his brother Leonard, running mills in Darwen and Preston. In 1893 he was elected on to the Town Council and was Mayor in 1903-1904 and Justice of the Peace in 1905. He was of an intellectual frame of mind and very knowledgeable on great works of literature. He was one of the founders of the Literary Society and became secretary and president. As Chairman of the Library Committee he was responsible for securing the aid of Andrew Carnegie in financing the building of the Library. In

politics he was an ardent Liberal and in religion he was a staunch Nonconformist with lifelong associations with Duckworth Street Congregational Church where he held many important offices. He married Eliza, the adopted daughter of Thomas Eccles and they lived at Earnsdale Cottage and then at Oldfield.

Earnsdale Cottage

Oldfield House

The End

Also Available from Heritage Publications

Darwen and its People by J. G. Shaw

A complete and definitive history of Darwen and its old families.

This book details the town's growth from the earliest times through to the late 1800s.

Paperback £15.99
Hardback £29.99

Available in 2013

The Houses of the Gentry in 19th Century Darwen
by L. Anne Hull

It can be seen by the number of large houses that Darwen was a prosperous town at the end of the 19th century. Many of the people who owned these houses contributed a great deal to the development of the town.

They were active in the Church and in politics and many showed a great interest in the welfare of their workers.

Also contains details of notable events in the history of Darwen in the 19th century.

Available from March 2013 for only £14.99 plus FREE postage or delivery.

Heritage
Publications

Call 01254 245709 or visit our website: www.HeritagePublications.co.uk